THE THIRD YPRES

PASSCHENDAELE

THE DAY-BY-DAY ACCOUNT

A shell-burst in the ruins of Boesinghe station, 17 August. The remains of a train can be seen in the distance. In the foreground is a shored up trench, in the riveting of which railway sleepers have been used. (Q.5890)

THE THIRD YPRES

PASSCHENDAELE

THE DAY-BY-DAY ACCOUNT

Chris McCarthy

ARMS AND
ARMOUR

Arms & Armour Press
An imprint of the Cassell Group
Wellington House, 125 Strand, London WC2R 0BB

Distributed in the USA by Sterling Publishing Co. Inc.,
387 Park Avenue South, New York, NY 10016-8810

Distributed in Australia by Capricorn Link (Australia) Pty Ltd,
2/13 Carrington Road, Castle Hill, New South Wales 2154

British Library Cataloguing-in-Publication data:
A catalogue record for this book is available from the British Library.

ISBN 1 85409 217 0

Edited and designed by Roger Chesneau/DAG Publications Ltd

Printed and bound in Great Britain

CONTENTS

PREFACE

Anyone who has ever tried to study 'Third Ypres' will know how difficult it is to gain a comprehensive picture of the battle from the British perspective, not least because there was little published in the months and years immediately following which dealt with troop movements along the entire front line. Individual unit histories, of which there are many, tended, naturally enough, to dwell on the exploits of the unit's own soldiers and rarely did more than sketch in the actions of its neighbours. In this book, therefore, I have attempted to draw together the various unit accounts to provide an overall picture of the major infantry movements and actions on a day-by-day basis. There were individual days when nothing much happened to affect the course of the battle as a whole, and I have chosen to state exactly that. This is not to say that local patrols, skirmishes and raids did not take place or that reliefs were not carried out on those days: I refer the reader to my notes on the latter below.

I have done my best to identify any mistakes that may have crept in and I apologize for those I might have missed. Any corrections for possible future editions are welcomed.

The following offers some general points on Third Ypres and explains some of the conventions used in the text:

Description of the action: As is customary, the action has been described from the right to the left of the line. The units are therefore organized in this order.

Use of tanks in the battle: Whilst, potentially, a number of tanks were available to support the infantry, weather conditions were often less than favourable and the tanks are mentioned in contemporary accounts only when the infantry felt they were of assistance. I have echoed this treatment here.

Divisional· reliefs: On average, it took three days to relieve a division in the line and, generally, I have used the day on which the relief began as the point of reference. However, on occasion, when a relief was the most significant event of the day, the median point has been used.

Weather: Details have been compiled partly from archives at the Meteorological Office (for general weather conditions) and partly from the Weather Diary of GHQ papers at the Public Records Office (for rainfall and temperature). The Meteorological Office records cover large areas of the Belgian battlefields and may not reflect very localized conditions. The Royal Engineers took temperature and rainfall readings twice a day at regular intervals but the times are not specified in the GHQ Diaries. I have therefore calculated the total rainfall for the day, and for the temperature I have used the highest figure. The weather station was located at Vlamertinghe, some 3.5 kilometres west of Ypres.

Terminology: The words 'Farm' and 'House' are often used interchangeably on maps and in written material of the time, as are the terms 'blockhouse' and 'pillbox', and I have followed this

trend. Interestingly, the German term for blockhouse was *Mannschaftseisenbetonunterstand*, which translates as 'reinforced concrete personnel shelter' and is occasionally seen elsewhere in the abbreviated form 'MEBU' or the anglicized plural 'MEBUs'.

Victoria Crosses: Sixty-one VCs were awarded during Third Ypres (including one bar to the VC), fifteen of them posthumously. Footnotes identify VC winners by name in the body of the text, and a full chronological listing appears in Appendix 3 complete with rank, unit, date and place of deed. Whilst the actions associated with VCs are momentous events in the lives of the individuals or in the annals of their units, in the context of this book they do not always feature large. Indeed, in the text I have chosen not to describe the specific deeds for which they were won, for to do so would be at odds with the rest of the book. Instead, footnotes have been placed at the first appropriate point on the day in question: if the relevant battalion is present in the text the footnote is attached to the first mention of it; if not the battalion, then the division is used, and so on down to the date itself. Some VCs were won for deeds carried out over a period of several days, and in these cases the first day has been selected.

Maps: Whilst every attempt has been made to mark accurately divisional boundaries, objectives and ground gained, these should be used only as a guide as unit accounts frequently provide conflicting information. This is not particularly surprising since, at the time, troops often had only the vaguest idea where they were in the moonscape of the battlefield, when fighting was at its height. In all cases I have used trench maps from my own collection and, as such, they span the general period of the battle whilst not necessarily illustrating a particular action. For this reason, important features and places may not have been marked on the original map, but I have added them where possible.

Photographs: All the photographs used in this book are from the Imperial War Museum's archives. The reference numbers in the captions identify the IWM negative numbers and the prefix letters indicate to which official collection they belong, e.g. 'E[Aus]' for Australia, 'CO' for Canada and 'Q' for British & General. Prints can be ordered from the Department of Photographs by quoting both the prefix and the number.

ACKNOWLEDGEMENTS

I should like to thank John Lee for contributing one of the most accessible introductions to the battle I have read, and my friends and colleagues at the Imperial War Museum, especially Jane Carmichael, Keeper of the Department of Photographs, for the use of the Collection; Phil Dutton; Mike Hibberd; Bryn Hammond; and Pete Simkins. I am grateful, too, to Mick Wood of the Archive Department at the Meteorological Office in Bracknell. Thanks are also due to the other members of the SHLM Battle Assessment project not already mentioned above, especially Gary Sheffield, Tony Cowan, Andy Simpson, Robin Brodhurst and Nick Perry. Finally, I am indebted to Kate Mazur, without whose help and support this book would not have seen the light of day.   **Chris McCarthy**

INTRODUCTION

JOHN LEE

More than for any other battle on the Western Front, with the possible exception of the first day of the Battle of the Somme, we need a re-assessment of the fighting which is officially referred to as 'Third Ypres' but which will be known for all time as 'Passchendaele', such is the redolence of that doom-laden name. It is to be regretted that the difficult conditions which brought the campaign to a dreary and desolate end so completely dominate the whole proceedings of an army that had improved enormously since its great test on the Somme the previous year.

Flanders had always been Sir Douglas Haig's preferred battleground. It was much nearer to his bases of supply, and an attack there promised more important strategic results. The demands of coalition warfare, and of domestic politics, had seen him tied to French strategy since he took command of the British Expeditionary Force in December 1915. Neither the Somme in 1916 nor Arras in 1917 were battles of first choice for the BEF. The complete failure of the Nivelle offensive in Champagne left Haig free to pursue his own strategy for the first time.

The army at his disposal in mid 1917 had learnt enormous and important lessons during the long campaign on the Somme and Ancre, which had been put to good use in the battles of April and May 1917—the three battles of the Scarpe known collectively as 'Arras', of which only the spectacular storming of Vimy Ridge is well known. The infantry now fought in platoons divided into four specialist sections, capable of sophisticated fire-and-movement tactics. The artillery had improved almost beyond recognition in terms of numbers of guns (in both field and heavy categories), the quantity and the reliability of shells and their

Shelled ground over which the troops advanced for the Passchendaele attack. Note the blockhouses in the background. February 1918. (Q.10498)

fuzes, and the perfection of its tactics. The staff work and general administration of the Army had undergone plenty of experiences to iron out many of the problems that beset it during the period of rapid, huge and unprecedented expansion from 1914 to 1916.

As a preliminary to the offensive, General Plumer was given the task of clearing the Germans off the Messines ridge, for which his Second Army had been preparing for nearly two years. The attack on 7 June 1917, made famous by the exploding of nineteen mines under the German positions, achieved this important preliminary, but the fighting beyond the ridge dragged on for another week before it was called off. Operations were stood down for six weeks while the centre of gravity was shifted to the north, where Sir Hubert Gough's Fifth Army was to conduct the offensive out of the Ypres salient. This was an unfortunate command decision on the part of Sir Douglas Haig.

The loss of six weeks of good campaigning weather was to prove particularly unlucky, but this could not be foreseen and there was a great task of preparation to be undertaken by the Fifth Army—guns to be moved, ammunition to be stockpiled, troops to be trained and rehearsed, plans to be perfected. The real problem was in taking the battle away from the meticulous Plumer and his staff, who 'knew every puddle' in the salient, and handing the battle over to the young 'thruster', Gough. Haig obviously thought that the offensive, if it was to achieve the great things he expected of it, needed the spirit that Gough would bring to the battle. But, at the same time, the staff officers of General Headquarters fully understood that the deep German defences on this sector would have to be worn down in a series of tremendous and carefully prepared battles. This dichotomy between the desire for a breakthrough and the need for a 'wearing down' fight was not resolved

in the planning meetings before 31 July. Gough failed to pay sufficient attention to the key to the enemy defences, the Gheluvelt plateau, and instead planned a deep penetration of the lines due north, over Pilckem Ridge and on towards the Passchendaele–Staden Ridge, the last high ground before the open country towards the railway centre of Roulers and the Belgian coast beyond.

On 31 July, behind a tremendous creeping barrage, the attack began. The enemy outpost line was swiftly overrun and the British pushed forward for a mile before enemy resistance stiffened significantly. In difficult fighting the advance continued, except on the right against the Gheluvelt plateau. In the afternoon the real nature

A wounded man is lifted from _Ernest_ ('G' Tank Battalion, 39th Division) into a Ford motor ambulance (No 13, belonging to the 3rd Division) near St Julien, 27 September. (Q.3548)

A German constructing a concrete observation post near Ypres, May 1917. (Q.45243)

of the German defensive scheme was revealed. The attackers, disorganized by the deep outpost line and the pill-boxes and strongpoints of the main line of resistance, and harried by the artillery massed beyond Gheluvelt, were now struck by the specially trained counter-attack divisions. All forward movement was halted; in places the attackers were pushed back. And then the heavens opened. Rain fell in torrents. The worst weather in Belgium for seventy-five years was to make the preceding good weather seem like a cruel joke. The first stage of the campaign ended as the battlefield turned into a swamp.

The British divisions were enduring appalling conditions and exhausting labours to keep their line occupied and supplied. It was to be 10 August before any further attack was possible, when the village of Westhoek was the only prize of the day. As the rain continued and the mud got worse, more and more divisions were being drawn into the Fifth Army to keep up its offensive capability. The next major effort, the Battle of Langemarck on 16 August, was a most comprehensive defeat for the weary attackers. The morale of the British Army reached possibly its lowest point in the war in this period of expensive and unproductive attacks to 'improve the line' before Gough's next big attack. But the Germans had other ideas and launched one of their 'deliberate' counter-attacks to regain the Inverness Copse area.

On that day Haig handed the battle back to Plumer and his Second Army. Plumer's incomparable staff presented a detailed plan for a series of 'bite and hold' battles to seize the Gheluvelt plateau and the Broodseinde and Passchendaele ridges. Plumer requested, and got, a three-week period to perfect his arrangements. The in-

fantry rehearsed their task until every man knew what was expected of him. The artillery planned a devastating, thousand-yard-deep creeping barrage to carry them over their objectives, and three separate standing barrages to protect them as they consolidated. But the real innovation on 20 September, the Battle of the Menin Road Ridge, was that the advance was to be strictly limited to what was within the capability of the attack formations, and the Germans were to be allowed to make their routine counter-attacks against British divisions dug in and waiting for them, protected by the carefully planned fire of artillery and machine guns. The battle, allowing for local setbacks against particularly strong defences, was a crushing victory in the main. British morale soared after such a clear-cut success against an overconfident enemy.

On 26 September Plumer delivered the second of his assaults, on a day noted for its hot, dry conditions—not exactly the popular image of the Passchendaele campaign. Further important sections of the enemy defences were wrested from them and, more importantly, the counter-attacks were thoroughly smashed. The British were beginning to consume German divisions faster than they could be relieved

and replaced. This was Haig's *raison d'être* for fighting it out in Flanders.

Ludendorff and the German generals were aghast at this development. Their new defence-in-depth tactics were being used against them very effectively by the master tactician, Plumer. Ludendorff could only order a more determined defence of the main line of resistance and a closing up of the counter-attack divisions for a quicker response. They launched a frenzied series of counter-attacks at the end of September and the beginning of October, which were pulverized by British artillery and machine-gun fire. Indeed, when Plumer's next assault began on 4 October, the British hurricane bombardment achieved complete surprise and caught masses of German troops in the open as they prepared another counter-attack. The Battle of Broodseinde Ridge was another punishing defeat for the Germans—one of those 'black days' that they record in their histories of the war. The powerful defences of the *Flandern I* line had been overwhelmed.

Haig began to order the cavalry divisions forward—a sure sign that he was expecting the enemy to collapse at any moment and allow the break-out into open country. Both Plumer and Gough, whose Fifth Army had been

The chaplain and Medical Officer at a regimental aid post of the South African Scottish in a captured German pillbox. (Q.11666)

conforming to the controlled advances of the Second Army, argued that such ideas were premature and that further attacks with limited objectives were required to secure the final ridge.

Sadly, the weather had broken again: heavy rain fell from 4 October. The ground became sodden, the efficacy of the British artillery bombardments declined, the very gun platforms became unstable and the infantry found movement extremely difficult. The Battle of Poelcappelle was only a partial success, with better results on the Fifth Army front than on that of the Second Army. The British put their lack of success down to the weather and failed to note that the German deployment of barbed wire had taken a qualitative leap forward, which should have been taken into account in future planning. As the rain continued the slightest movement became an ordeal: this is the classic period of the 'sea of mud' for which the campaign is remembered.

The First Battle of Passchendaele fought on 12 October was a pale imitation of the September successes. Mud negated the bombardment and slowed the infantry to a crawl. Very little ground was gained. During the rain-enforced pause the Canadian Corps was brought up to the Salient for the last major effort to secure the crest of the Passchendaele–Staden ridge. The Second Battle of Passchendaele, on 26 October, again saw little reward for great effort.

The Italian disaster at Caporetto now impinged on the British campaign in Flanders. Haig was peremptorily ordered to send British divisions to restore the situation in Italy. The 23rd and 41st Divisions left immediately and the 5th, 7th and 48th Divisions soon followed. Plumer was sent to command them. There was no hope now of decisive results in 1917. Two further efforts by Canadian and British troops in November dragged the exhausted infantry on to the highest points of the

ridge, without securing it all. The campaign was finally, belatedly, wound up.

There are many tantalizing questions about the handling of the campaign. What if the delay between the end of the Battle of Messines and the start of Third Ypres had been less than six weeks? What if the opening battles had been fought on the same principles as Plumer later employed? What if the weather had not been so unpredictably awful? Haig chose Gough to handle the offensive. Gough remained completely unapologetic about his early conduct of the campaign, insisting that limited objectives meant the loss of initiative and a failure to grasp fleeting opportunities. He had clearly failed to grasp the significance of the new German defence tactics, however, which invited attackers to over-extend themselves, leaving them a disorganized prey to the specially trained *Eingreif* divisions.

Critics point to the British casualties of nearly a quarter of a million men and the demonstrable failure to break through the German defences and clear the Belgian coast of the U-boat menace. But this is to take a very one-sided view of the campaign. The Germans considered the autumn 1917 battles an unmitigated disaster. In the diaries of the Bavarian Crown Prince Rupert, the army group commander with overall responsibility for the battle, and of several chiefs of staff involved, the entries record the ruination of the best divisions of the German Army on the Western Front. In all, 88 divisions— over half of the total serving in France and Flanders—were drawn into the battle and thoroughly pulverized. All the tactical innovation and preparation of the best brains of the Great General Staff could not prevent the methodical British gouging chunks out of the defences and inflicting appalling casualties on the defenders and counter-attackers. The German Army had to endure the most punishing ordeal at the hands of the British artillery, which increased in power and efficiency dramatically throughout the war from 1916 to 1918. The delayed and faulty start to the campaign, and the fortuitous early break in the weather, together with the more predictably bad later weather, was what prevented an even greater catastrophe for the German Army. It was the prospect of facing yet more punishing battles of attrition against a materially stronger Allied coalition that encouraged Ludendorff to stake everything on the offensives of 1918—which eventually cost Germany the war.

The other important consideration which should be taken into account by military historians is the condition of the French Army during this period. The hopes of a decisive victory inspired by Robert Nivelle before the great offensive in Champagne that bears his name made the costly failure there a particularly bitter blow to the long-suffering *poilus*. The refusal of some divisions to return to the front line after a period of rest soon spread through the French Army until large sections of it could not be relied upon. There was never any real question that they would refuse to fight if the Germans attacked, though perhaps the French ruling class could be forgiven for fearing the same, given the agitation sweeping their Russian allies at that time. There can be no doubt that the unrelenting pressure kept up by the British at Ypres tied the Germans completely to that theatre of operations. The Germans were never able to discover the real weakness of the French or devise any way of turning it to their advantage. This has to be counted as a 'plus' factor for the Allies when assessing the campaign.

Chris McCarthy has already produced a book which all visitors to and students of the 1916 battles of the Somme find very valuable. He will not mind it being described as a useful reworking of the two volumes of the official history of the campaign. But in this new book on Third Ypres he has added enormously to our knowledge of the autumn 1917 campaign. The single volume of the Official History was very late, very controversial and quite inadequate. It passed over large-scale fighting with the briefest of references, made several factual errors and was very ill-served by its maps. We should all be very grateful for the detailed research that has gone into the current work, in which the new maps are particularly impressive and valuable.

Australian and German dead at Stirling Castle—the result of shellfire. The photograph is dated 20 September. (E[AUS].4677)

11th Durham Light Infantry (Pioneers, 20 Div.) are taken forward by light railway. Here they are passing Elverdinghe, 31 July. (Q.2641)

JULY

Tuesday 31 July

Temperature 69°F; overcast. Rainfall: 21.7mm.

BATTLE OF PILCKEM RIDGE (31 July–2 August)

SECOND ARMY

II ANZAC Corps
New Zealand Division

1 NZ Brigade: At 3.50 a.m., zero hour, the 1st Auckland raided the northern sector of the Divisional front, with the 2nd Auckland in support. The 2nd Wellington[1] were to attack La Basse-Ville.

The Wellingtons met with strong resistance. The Refinery was captured and two platoons worked their way through the village, which was cleared in half an hour with bomb and bayonet. An *estaminet* on the Warneton road called Der Rooster Cabaret was cleared by a patrol but not held. The 2nd Platoon had the difficult task of clear-

German prisoners waiting to be interrogated at Pilckem, 31 July. (Q.5724)

ing the hedgerows: they attacked under cover of a five-minute barrage by light trench mortars and Lewis guns and, whilst suffering severe casualties initially, cleared the hedgerows and consolidated the position.

The 1st Auckland attacked a series of fortified shell holes. They were divided into three parties. On the right the defenders either ran or were shot down. The centre party's experience was similar, but, on the left, the third party was stopped by three machine guns and a trench mortar bombardment.

A counter-attack was launched from the direction of Der Rooster Cabaret but was destroyed by artillery and small-arms fire. The New Zealanders repelled a second counter-attack, during the course of which twenty Germans were shot and thirteen bayoneted. A third counter-attack in the evening was dealt with by artillery and small-arms fire.

3rd Australian Division

The Division attacked at 3.50 a.m., zero hour, with one brigade.

11 Australian Brigade, with the 43rd and 42nd Battalions, attacked a series of German outposts numbered III–VII (from the north), only 100 yards from their front line.

The 43rd Battalion joined with the enemy almost straightaway and sharp fights with bomb and rifle ensued. The Windmill, which was now a heap of rubble, held out for a while but was charged and finally captured. The 42nd Battalion also successfully took their objective, after opposition at posts VIII and IX had been cleared. Within a quarter of an hour the attacking wave had reached the wire of the Warneton Line. On the extreme right flank, post XV, just outside the attack, was firing into the flank of the 43rd. The troops attacking post XIV went on and captured it.

Around dusk, at 8 p.m., when the attacking battalions were about to be relieved by the 41st Battalion, the Germans counter-attacked and recaptured the Windmill. The 43rd, however, recaptured the post at 12.30 a.m. on 1 August and the position was consolidated.

IX Corps
37th Division

63 Brigade attacked initially with the 4th Middlesex and 8th Lincolns under the command of the 19th Division, then with the 10th Yorks & Lancs and the 8th Somerset Light Infantry under the command of the 37th Division. The 8th East Lancs (112 Brigade) were also attached.

At 3.50 a.m., zero hour, the 4th Middlesex, in conjunction with the 19th Division, advanced to the line of its objective, July Farm–Rifle Farm. On the right, a company of 8th Lincolns also advanced with its left on Rifle Farm and its right thrown back to the British line, in touch with the 8th Somersets.

[1]VC: Cpl Leslie Wilton Andrew.

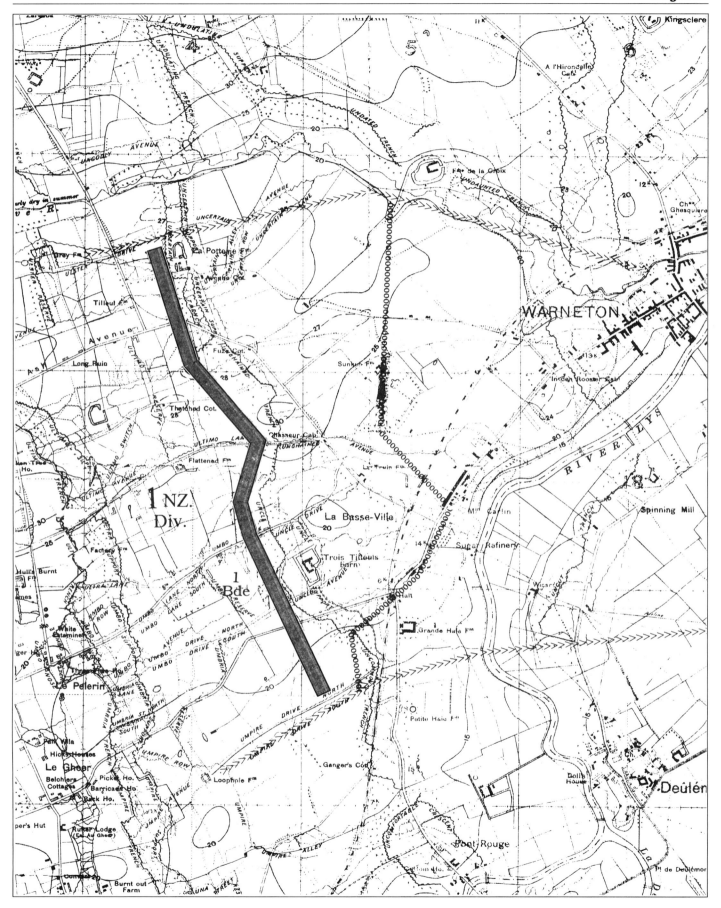

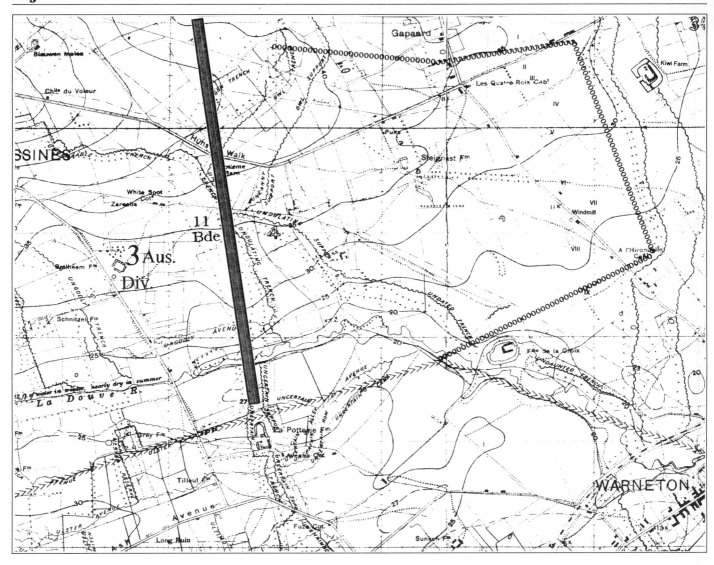

The second phase of the attack was launched at 7.50 a.m. with the Somersets and the Lincolns. They advanced to the western edge of Beek Farm and 'A' Company of the Somersets dug in. Two platoons of the Somersets went on to try to clear Beek Wood but were unsuccessful. Meanwhile Rifle Farm had fallen to a counter-attack, which forced the Lincolns to pull their left flank back to June Farm.

At 8 p.m. the enemy were seen massing for a counter-attack but were dealt with by artillery fire.

19th Division

56 Brigade attacked at 3.50 a.m., zero hour, with the 7th King's Own (R Lancs), 7th East Lancs and 7th North Lancs. The 7th South Lancs were in support.

The King's Own took all their objectives, including Junction Buildings and Tiny and Spider Farms. At 4.10 a.m. the right company was on the Blue Line, in touch with the 4th Middlesex (37th Division), although a 300-yard gap opposite Wasp Farm and Fly Buildings had opened between the companies. The rest of the Battalion was linked with the East Lancs west of Fly Buildings. The two right companies of the King's Own reached the Blue Line, with the East Lancs on the left. The North Lancs reached it with the two companies on the right, while the two left companies were thrown back southwest of Forret Farm, to make a flank.

At 6.46 a.m., under a smokescreen, the Germans counter-attacked the join between the divisions at Rifle Farm, which was recaptured. At 7.45 another counter-attack came from the direction of Fly Buildings. It was repulsed by the two companies on the left of the King's Own, but it forced the right companies back to Tiny Farm. The 9th Royal Welsh Fusiliers (58 Brigade) were sent up to form a defensive flank.

X Corps
41st Division

The Division attacked astride the Ysers–Comines Canal at 3.50 a.m., zero hour, with two brigades.
122 Brigade attacked south of the canal with the 18th King's Royal Rifle Corps

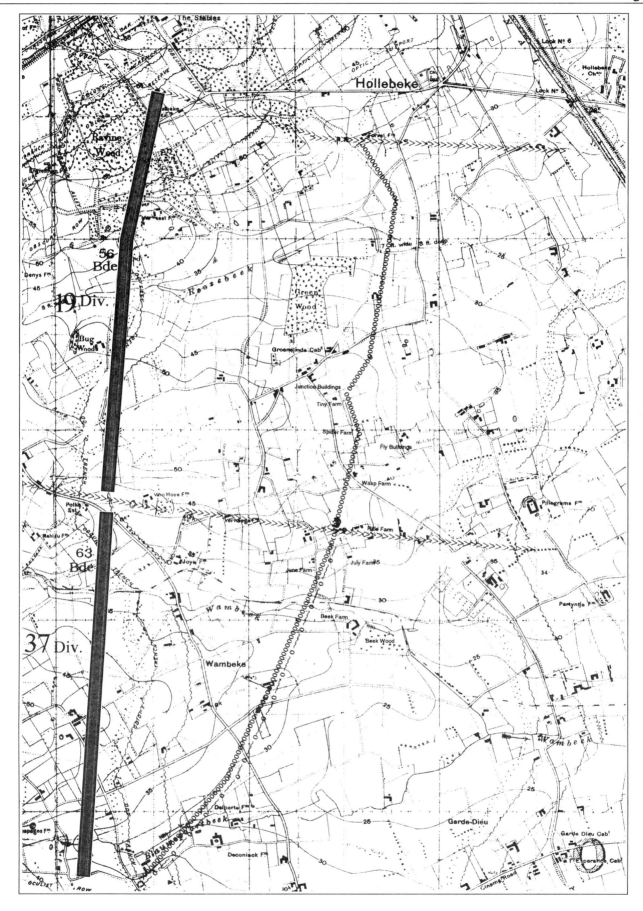

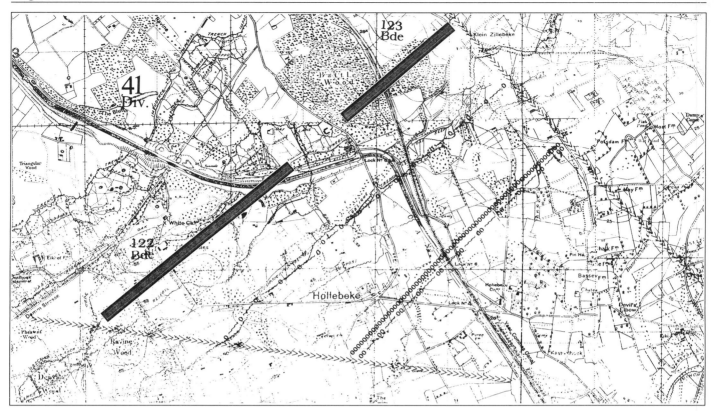

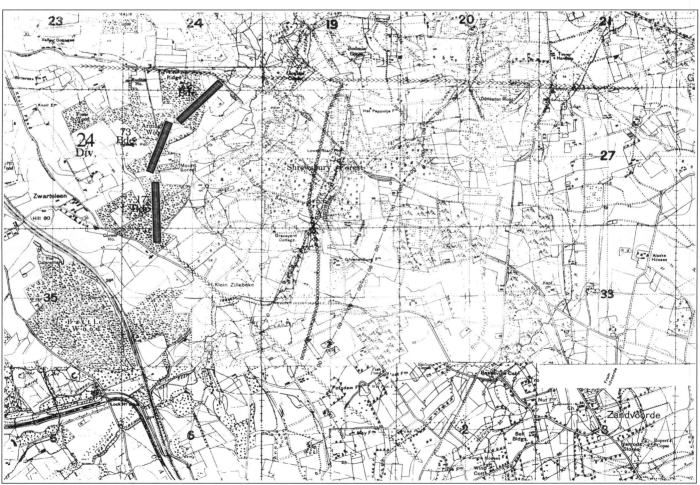

and 11th Royal West Kents, with the 12th East Surreys in support. After a fierce fight, Oblique Support Trench fell to the Royal West Kents. The attacking troops then came under fire from houses along the Hollebeke Road. The KRRC were held up by machine-gun fire from around Hollebeke Church. At 8 a.m. the Royal West Kents took up the attack on the village. They had cleared it by 11.30 a.m. and started to consolidate in the ruins. The final position was just 100 yards short of the final objective, the Green Line. That night the 12th East Surreys came up and pushed on to capture Forret Farm.

123 Brigade attacked north of the canal with two companies of the 23rd Middlesex, 11th Queen's, 10th Royal West Kents and 20th Durham Light Infantry in support. Despite meeting strong opposition they managed to take the first objective, the Red Line. Progress was slow owing to the state of the ground and the barrage which got ahead of the attacking troops. The Middlesex encountered flooded ground between the canal and the railway embankment, which forced them to advance along the embankment. By about 8 a.m. parties of the West Kents and Queen's had reached the second objective, the Blue Line, and consolidated. An attempt was made to take the Green Line, but a line of pillboxes resisted all attempts at capture. During the day parties from all the attacking troops filtered up and dug in.

FIFTH ARMY
II Corps
24th Division

The Division was to form a defensive flank. It attacked at 3.50 a.m., zero hour, with three brigades.

17 Brigade: The 1st Royal Fusiliers reached the Blue Line and joined with 73 Brigade in attacking Lower Star Post. The 12th Royal Fusiliers passed through the 1st and carried on towards the Black Line, where they came under fire from a strongpoint on the left flank and Tower Hamlets. The 12th Battalion reached to within 200 yards of the Bassevillebeek but was forced to withdraw to 300 yards short of the Blue Line. The 3rd Rifle Brigade on the right of the Brigade helped the Fusiliers to consolidate.

73 Brigade attacked through Shrewsbury Forest with the 7th Northants and 2nd Leinsters. They were held up by fighting in the forest but reached Jehovah Trench. The advance continued, taking Groenenburg Farm and

A dump of water-filled petrol tins at Elverdinghe, 31 July. (Q.5718)

capturing the flooded Jordan Trench, but it was stopped by the pillboxes at Lower Star Post. The enemy held out all day, preventing any further advance. 73 Brigade fell back and dug a line just in advance of Jehovah Trench. *72 Brigade*, using the 1st North Staffs and 8th Queen's for the assault, reached the Blue Line level with Bodmin Copse and then pushed on to the Black Line. They managed to reach Bassevillebeek at the foot of Dumbarton Wood, where they came under enfilade fire from the wood on the left and Lower Star Post on the right. They were forced to withdraw to south of Bodmin Copse, a few hundred yards short of their first objective, the Red Line.

30th Division

The Division attacked at 3.50 a.m., zero hour, with two brigades, plus one in support.

21 Brigade: The 2nd Green Howards were supported by the 19th Manchesters on the right and the 2nd Wiltshires on the left were supported by the 18th King's Liverpool Regiment.

The Brigade were held up in the assembly dug-outs by enemy shell-fire and they just missed the barrage. This caused confusion in the subsequent advance through Sanctuary Wood, with the result that the battalions became intermixed.

The leading companies of the 18th King's (1st and 3rd) pushed on, their right on Jar Row and their left on the tramway south of Stirling Castle. They advanced to just south of Stirling Castle. The 2nd and 4th Companies of the King's wandered off to the left and became involved with troops moving to the north-east. Some crossed the Menin Road at Clapham Junction, while others were at Stirling Castle.

In Jar Row itself a mixed force of Wiltshires, Manchesters and 2nd Scots Fusiliers (90 Brigade) attempted to bomb along the trench but were beaten back by enemy bombs and machine-gun fire. On leaving Sanctuary Wood they came under fire from machine guns at Stirling Castle, 500 yards to their front. They were unable to capture the Castle until reinforced by the 89th Brigade, who were in support. Bodmin Copse was taken.

90 Brigade: The 16th and 18th Manchesters took the Blue Line, while the 17th Manchesters passed through the 16th and consolidated just short of the second objective as severe machine-gun fire from Stirling Castle and the surrounding area held up any further advance.

The 2nd Royal Scots Fusiliers, on the left, lost direction in Sanctuary Wood, strayed north and, attacked

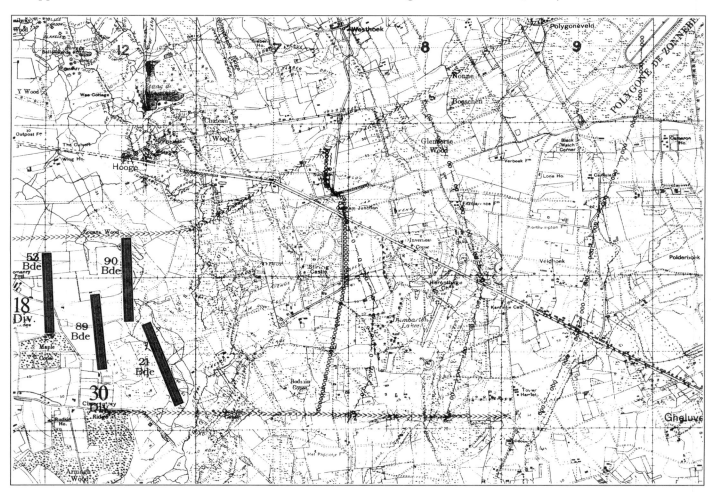

Château Wood (north of the Menin Road). Thinking it to be Glencorse Wood, they reported its capture to HQ.

89 Brigade: As planned, the Brigade advanced in support of 21 and 90 Brigades from Maple Copse, with the 20th King's Liverpool Regiment on the right and the 17th on the left. The 19th King's and 2nd Bedfords were in support; the 19th King's were to fill the gap between the 30th and 8th Divisions, across the Menin Road.

The 17th King's reached Stirling Castle at 8.40 a.m. to find that there were no British troops in front of them. With their left flank on Clapham Junction, they held a position east of Stirling Castle, roughly along the road south of Clapham Junction, overlooking Dumbarton Lakes. There they linked up with the 24th Brigade (8th Division).

The 19th King's and 2nd Bedfords were held at Maple Copse until required to relieve 53 Brigade (18th Division) at 10 p.m.

18th Division (in support of 30th Division)

53 Brigade: The Brigade's task was to leap-frog the 30th Division when the first objective, including Glencorse Wood, was taken.

By 8.10 a.m. the 8th Suffolks arrived in Jackdaw Reserve Trench, only to find that the western edge of Glencorse Wood was still held by the enemy. They advanced to the Menin Road, reaching it at 8.45 a.m. One company reached Surbiton Villas and dug in, while the rest of the Battalion bridged the gap between Surbiton Villas and Jap Avenue near Clapham Junction.

The 6th Berkshires, meanwhile, wrongly believing Glencorse Wood to be held by the British, met with intense machine-gun fire just short of the Menin Road. They co-opted sappers and pioneers of 79 Company Royal Engineers to help clear the pillboxes between the Menin Road and Glencorse Wood. As the fighting progressed, five tanks came up but became bogged down in the mud; four were finally knocked out by shell-fire. However, before 10 a.m. the Berkshires had taken Jargon Switch and the crossroads north-west of Glencorse Wood. To bridge the gap between the 30th and 8th Divisions, a strongpoint was dug and reinforced by a party of Manchesters (30th Division).

8th Division

The Division attacked at 3.50 a.m., zero hour, with two brigades, plus one in support.

---

[2]VC: Capt Thomas Riverdale Colyer-Fergusson.

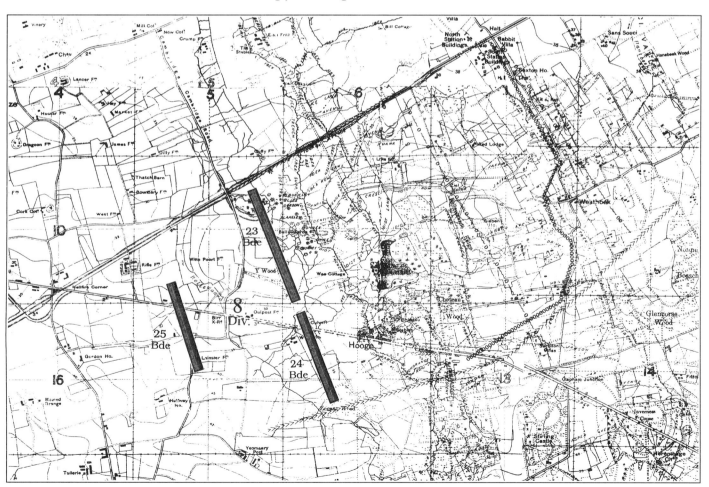

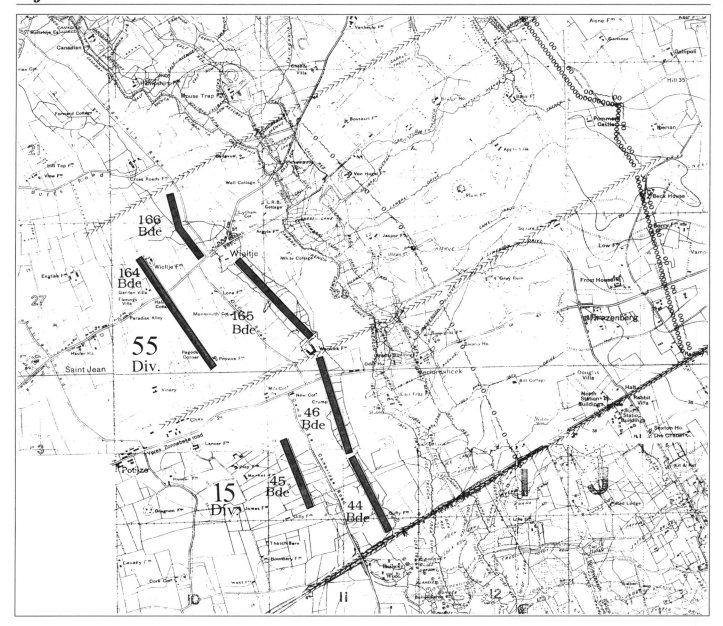

24 *Brigade* attacked with the 1st Worcesters and 2nd Northants[2]. The 2nd East Lancs and 1st Sherwood Foresters were to pass through and take the Black Line. With the aid of mortars firing thermite shells on the banks, Bellewaarde Lake was taken by the 2nd Northants. Beyond the lake, the barrage was nearly lost as the attacking troops struggled through the debris of Château Wood. The Blue Line, Jacob Trench and Bellewaarde Ridge were taken by the Worcesters and Northants, and the 1st Sherwood Foresters passed through them and on to the Black Line. There they came under machine-gun fire from Hanebeek valley some 700 yards away and from Glencorse Wood on the right flank, and the Brigade was pulled back to the shelter of Westhoek Ridge.

23 *Brigade* attacked with the 2nd West Yorks on the right and the 2nd Devonshires on the left. The Yorkshires went right through and captured the Blue Line, taking Ziel House on the way. The 2nd Scottish Rifles were in support and leap-frogged them to go on to take the Black Line and Jaffa Trench. On the way they received some rifle fire from the Kit and Kat blockhouses on the ridge, but this was dealt with by Lewis guns and rifle grenades.

The 2nd Devonshires on the left reached their objective, the Blue Line, having met little opposition. The 2nd Middlesex, in support, followed the Devons closely and passed through them to take the Black Line. However, as with 24 Brigade, machine-gun fire from Hanebeek valley and Glencorse Wood caused 23 Brigade to pull back to the shelter of Westhoek Ridge.

---

[3]VC: T/Brig-Gen Clifford Coffin, Commander.

25 Brigade[3], in support, attacked with the 2nd Lincolns, 1st Royal Irish Rifles and 2nd Rifle Brigade. To compensate for the 30th Division's failure on the right, a company of the 2nd Royal Berks were to form a defensive flank if needed. The 2nd Rifle Brigade established an outpost at Hanebeek Wood, but, owing to their exposed position, they withdrew to Kit and Kat. The Lincolns and Irish Rifles came under severe fire from the untaken Glencorse and Nonne Bosschen Woods. Parties from both battalions made isolated progress. It was decided to consolidate Jabber Trench with Lewis-gun posts on the crest of the ridge; the position was just short of the Black Line.

Before midday local counter-attacks were driven off. In two, more determined attacks launched by the Germans shortly after 2 p.m., pockets of ground were lost but immediately recaptured. The 2nd Middlesex were brought up to fill the gap that appeared between the Irish Rifles and the Rifle Brigade.

At around 5 p.m. the enemy started to form up at the bottom of Hanebeek valley, only to be dispersed by artillery and machine-gun fire.

XIX CORPS
15th Division

The Division attacked at 3.50 a.m., zero hour, with two brigades, plus one in support.

44 Brigade attacked with the 8/10th Gordon Highlanders[4] and 9th Black Watch; the 8th Seaforths were in support. The attacking troops reached the Blue Line with little loss and kept up with the barrage. They were in touch with the 8th Division (II Corps) on the right. The wire around Frezenburg and North Station Buildings was found to be well cut and, with the help of the one remaining tank (*Challenger*), the Black Watch and the Gordons fought their way through the village and on to the Black Line, where they consoli-

dated a line 500 yards east of the village. Two counter-attacks, one at 8.30 a.m. and another at 10 a.m., were fought off.

46 Brigade used the 7/8th King's Own Scottish Borderers and 10/11th Highland Light Infantry, with the 10th Scottish Rifles in support. The KOSB met strong resistance from a redoubt in Frezenburg village, but two tanks on either flank aided the attackers and they reached the Blue Line, where they reorganized. At 5 a.m. the attack continued, but it was held up by the Frezenburg Redoubt, astride the Ypres≈ Zonnebeke road. A party of KOSB eventually outflanked and captured it.

The HLI came under fire from Square Farm[5] and Hill 35 and enfilade fire from Frost House. (Square Farm subsequently fell to the 1/7th King's Liverpool Regiment, enabling the 55th Division, on the left, to get forward.) Moving on, the HLI took Low Farm but were checked by fire from Pommern Castle and Hill 35. It was 10 a.m. before they reached the Black Line.

Filling water-bottles at a well near Elverdinghe, 31 July. (Q.5719)

45 Brigade's task, in support, was to pass through and take the Green Line. It attacked on the Divisional front with the 6/7th Royal Scots Fusiliers and the 6th Camerons. The 11th Argyll & Sutherland Highlanders and the 13th Royal Scots were in support. The A&SH sent two platoons south of the railway to form a defensive flank between the 15th and 8th Divisions.

At 2 p.m. a counter-attack was launched at the Camerons and the 55th Division on their left. This was fought off, but 164 Brigade (55th Division), facing a second attack with both flanks exposed, withdrew to form a line from Pommern Castle along the ridge to Beck House. The 10/11th HLI were sent out to strengthen the left flank at Iberian Farm. That night the line was consolidated.

---

[4] 8 Bn amalgamated with 10 Bn on 11 May 1916 to form 8/10th Gordon Highlanders.
[5] Square Farm was a large, fortified ruin with vaulted cellars, situated in a belt of strongpoints.

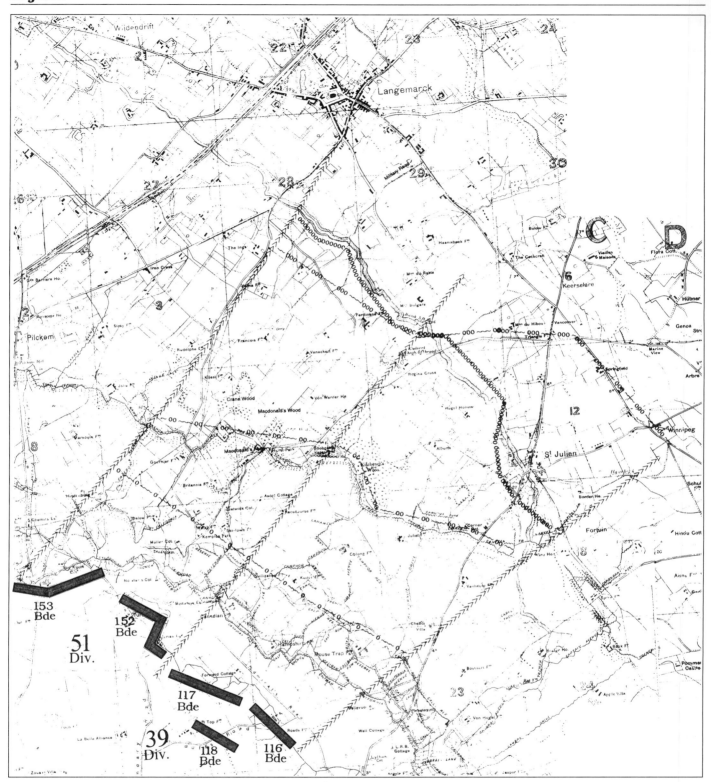

55th Division

The Division attacked at 3.50 a.m., zero hour, with two brigades, plus one in support.

165 Brigade: The 1/5th and 1/6th King's Liverpool Regiment advanced to the Blue Line with little trouble. Enemy machine guns were found to be very active from Plum Farm, located well beyond the Blue Line: it was immediately attacked and taken whilst the barrage still played on it.

The attack was taken up by the 1/7th and 1/9th King's Liverpool Regiment. The 1/7th were delayed by Square Farm in the 15th Division's area. This held up several attacks until finally falling to the 1/7th, who took

150 prisoners. The Brigade advanced and went on to take their section of the Black Line, though Pommern Redoubt held out in places until 9 a.m. and Bank Farm held out until a tank arrived to clear it.

166 Brigade, attacking with the 1/5th King's Own (R Lancs) and the 1/5th North Lancs, encountered a number of machine-gun nests on the way but managed to keep up with the barrage. The attack was taken over by the 1/10th Liverpool Scottish[6] and the 1/5th South Lancs, who experienced strong opposition from Spree Farm, Capricorn Trench and the distant Pond Farm, south-east of St Julien. The 1/5th North Lancs were sent in support.

By 7 a.m. the Liverpool Scottish were in complete control of Capricorn Trench and in touch with the 1/5th South Lancs. Whilst it was reported that the whole of the Black Line was taken, Spree Farm and Pond Farm had not in fact fallen and caused considerable casualties.

164 Brigade: At 10.10 a.m. the Brigade advanced to capture the final objective, the Green Line. Spree Farm fell to the 2/5th Lancashire Fusiliers[7], who had the 1/8th Liverpool Irish in support. The 1/4th North Lancs, supported by the 1/4th King's Own (R Lancs)[8], successfully advanced to the Green Line, capturing five batteries of 77mm guns on the way. Contact was made with the 15th Division on the right and visual contact with the 118th Brigade (39th Division) on the left, who were around the distant Wurst Farm and Aviatik. Later, news that the 118th Brigade had been forced back to Border House on the Black Line caused the 164th Brigade in turn to bend their line back in order to keep touch.

XVIII CORPS
39th Division

The Division attacked at 3.50 a.m., zero hour, with two brigades, plus one in support. With the aid of eight tanks,

it captured the Blue Line with little trouble.

116 Brigade consisted of the 11th, 12th and 13th Royal Sussex and the 14th Hampshire Regiment[9]. Aided by two tanks which knocked out a battery of artillery, the 13th Royal Sussex captured St Julien and took prisoner seventeen officers and 205 other ranks.

117 Brigade attacked with the 16th Sherwood Foresters and the 17th King's Royal Rifle Corps; the 16th Rifle Brigade and 17th Sherwood Foresters, in support, passed through. Using Stokes mortars and rifle grenades as a local barrage, they rushed and took the three pillboxes at Regina Cross. Alberta, another centre of resistance, also fell.

118 Brigade set out at 8 a.m. with the 1/6th Cheshires, 1/1st Hertfordshires and 4/5th Black Watch; the 1/1st Cambridgeshires were in support. The Black Watch, on the left, advanced with little difficulty through Kitchener's Wood and across the Steenbeek. On the right, the Cheshires passed through St Julien. The Hertfordshires, however, were cut down by machine-gun fire.

The Brigade advanced on the right as far as Von Tirpitz Farm. However, the 55th Division, on the right, had not come up and the flank was exposed to enfilade fire. The 118th Brigade thus suffered from heavy counter-attacks, forcing them to withdraw from St Julien to the east bank of the Steenbeek. They were then withdrawn to Divisional Reserve and the line from St Julien to the Culvert was held by the 116th and 117th Brigades, where they linked with the 51st Division.

51st Division

The Division attacked at 3.50 a.m., zero hour, with two brigades, plus one in reserve. A trench mortar barrage consisting of cans of burning oil was employed.[10]

152 Brigade attacked with the 1/5th Seaforth Highlanders and the 1/8th Argyll & Sutherland Highlanders. They

reached the Blue Line, meeting with little resistance from the Germans. The 1/6th Seaforths[11] and 1/6th Gordon Highlanders[12] took over the advance. The Gordons encountered opposition from Ascot Cottage but took it with the help of a passing tank and continued on to the Black Line. A party was detailed to link up with the Seaforths and join in an attack on Macdonald's Farm and Wood. Tank G50 fired six rounds into the farm, helping to weaken the enemy's resolve, and the position fell. The Gordons continued to the Green Line until stopped by machine-gun fire from the other side of the Steenbeek, and dug in 100 yards from the stream.

153 Brigade consisted of the 1/7th Gordon Highlanders and the 1/7th Black Watch. The Gordons took Hindenburg Farm on the way to the Blue Line; the Black Watch came upon the remains of an elaborate trench system but went on to the Blue Line.

Continuing with the 1/5th Gordons and the 1/6th Black Watch, in support, the attack encountered a pocket of strong resistance from a row of pillboxes. These were outflanked and taken, allowing the Gordons to move on to the Black Line. Little resistance was encountered on their progression to the Green Line and they eventually occupied a line 200 yards south-west of the Steenbeek, taking, on the way, a blockhouse near François Farm and, with the 38th Division, Varna Farm. They dug in on the Green Line.

[6]VC: Capt Noel Godfrey Chavasse.
[7]VC: T/Lt-Col Bertram Best Dunkley, Commander.
[8]VC: L-Sgt Tom Fletcher Mayson.
[9]VC: Lt Dennis George Wyldbore Hewitt.
[10]Eight tanks supported the attack. Their fates were as follows: G49 stuck at the Blue Line; G41 stuck 200 yards beyond the Blue Line; G51 reached Kitchener's Wood; G44, G45 and G52 reached the Green Line, having dealt with several machine guns; G50 reached Varna Farm after several engagements; and G42 reached the Black Line and worked along it.
[11]VC: Sgt Alexander Edwards.
[12]VC: Pte George Imlach McIntosh.

The Black Watch were checked by machine-gun fire from Goumier Farm. This was cleared and they went on to the Black Line. Continuing with the attack, they encountered heavy fire from Rudolphe Farm and Cane Wood. Parties were sent out across a bridge over the Steenbeek, north of the Military Road, where posts were established. This was the signal for a squadron of King Edward's Horse to advance and patrol north of the Steenbeek. However, they came under heavy machine-gun fire and dug in, covering Maison du Rasta.

A counter-attack was launched between 3 and 4 p.m. but was stopped by small-arms fire. Taking advantage of the confusion, the 1/6th Seaforths and the 1/8th A&SH (152 Brigade) crossed the stream and dug in opposite Ferdinand Farm. They then rushed Maison du Rasta and established posts there and at Maison Bulgare. After another counter-attack it was decided to pull all troops back to south of the Steenbeek, holding only the bridges.

164 Brigade, in reserve, were not employed.

XIV CORPS
38th Division

The Division attacked at 3.50 a.m., zero hour, with two brigades, plus one in support.

114 Brigade: The 10th and 13th Welsh Regiment captured the Blue Line with little difficulty. The attack was taken up by the 15th Welsh on the right and the 14th Welsh on the left. Stiff opposition was met in the vicinity of Iron Cross, which eventually fell to the 14th Welsh. The 15th Royal Welsh Fusiliers, in their advance from the Blue Line, came under heavy artillery fire and lost the barrage. However, they struggled on to the Iron Cross Ridge. The Green Line was attacked by half-battalions of the 14th and 15th Welsh Regiment on the right and by the 15th Royal Welsh Fusiliers on the left. They came under fire from Rudolphe Farm in the 51st Division's area. A platoon of the 15th Welsh Regiment was detailed to take it, and did so.

113 Brigade: The 13th Royal Welsh Fusiliers[13] (two companies) and the 16th Royal Welsh Fusiliers met resistance from Marsouin and Stray Farms on the right and the village of Pilckem on

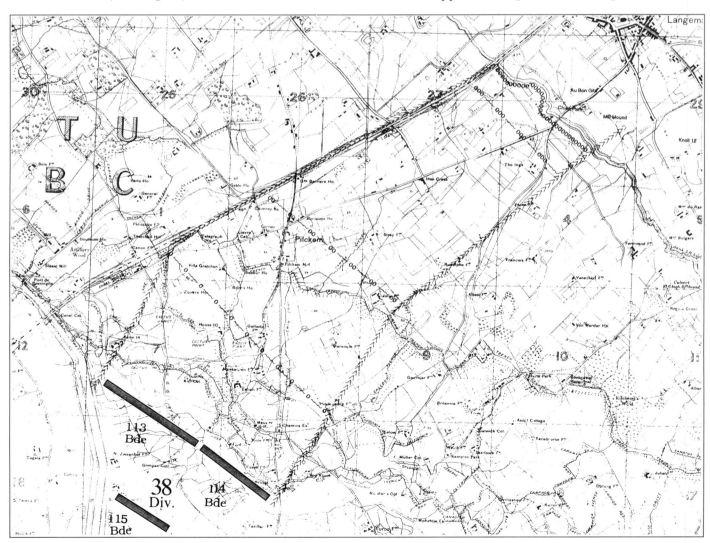

the left but finally reached the Black Line.

115 Brigade (in support): Whilst 113 and 114 Brigades were attacking Iron Cross Ridge, the 11th South Wales Borderers[14] and the 17th Royal Welsh Fusiliers were moving up in support to take up the attack on the Steenbeek. Most houses along the top of the ridge had been converted into concrete machine-gun posts: these held up the troops facing them, whilst others on the flanks pushed forward and took them in the rear. The houses fell and the Steenbeek was crossed. A company of the 10th South Wales Borderers reinforced the Fusiliers.

The Germans counter-attacked at 3.10 p.m. and were repulsed except at Au Bon-Gite, where a party of 11th South Wales Borderers were driven back across the Steenbeek to the west bank. Another attempt was made by the enemy later in the afternoon but was driven off by artillery fire.

Guards Division

The Division attacked at 3.50 a.m., zero hour, with two brigades, plus one in support.

2 Guards Brigade: The 1st Scots Guards advanced to the Blue Line, meeting little resistance, as did the 2nd Irish Guards, who arrived at the Blue Line within fifteen minutes of leaving their jump-off point. Whilst consolidating the Blue Line, the Scots came under fire from Artillery Wood but this was dealt with by artillery fire.

At 5 a.m. the Brigade continued its advance to the Black Line. The Scots again met little opposition, but the Irish came under heavy fire from Hey Wood. They managed to reach the Black Line, however, by 6 a.m.

3 Guards Brigade: The 1st Grenadier Guards and the 1st Welsh Guards[15] also made the Blue Line with no problem, apart from coming under fire from a blockhouse in Wood 15; this was cleared. Touch was maintained with the French on the left, and the advance to the Black Line continued with no major hold up.

The attack on the Green Line was taken up by the supporting battalions of 2 and 3 Guards Brigades at 7.15 a.m. On the right of 2 Guards Brigade, the 3rd Grenadier Guards came under machine-gun fire from blockhouses on

The Battle of Pilckem Ridge: British soldiers of the Guards Division in the new support line after the first objectives had been taken, 31 July. (Q.2627)

the Ypres≈Staden railway line. This also affected the advance of 38th Division. However, by 8 a.m., with the blockhouses taken, they were able to drive the enemy back from Vulcan Crossing on the join with the 38th Division.

The 1st Coldstream Guards[16] were forced to extend their left flank to support the right of 3 Guards Brigade, which had been checked at Abri Wood. The wood was cleared with the help of a smokescreen, however, and they pushed on and took Fourche and Captain's Farms, where they consolidated their position.

The 2nd Scots Guards, on the extreme left and in close touch with the 201st French Regiment, met little opposition and took their objective with little difficulty.

[13]VC: Cpl James Llewellyn Davies.
[14]VC: Sgt Ivor Rees.
[15]VC: Sgt Robert James Bye.
[16]VC: Pte Thomas Whitham.

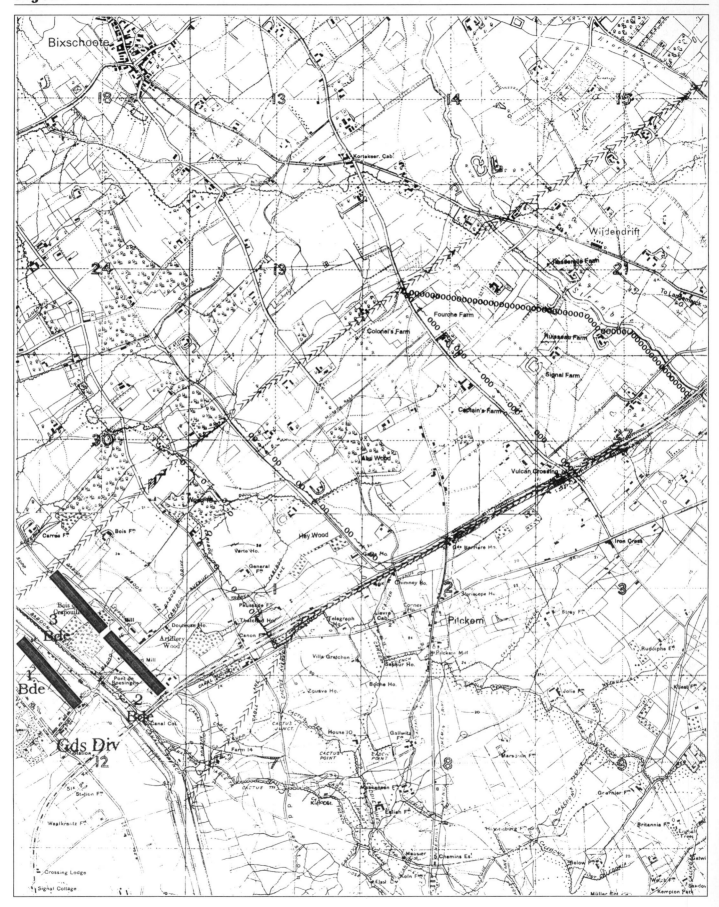

The Guards Division crosses the Yser Canal at Boesinghe, 31 July. The pouch on the bridle of the mule contains a gas mask. (Q.2635)

Dressing the wound of Lt Guy Vaughan Morgan, 2nd Bn Irish Guards, at a dressing station at Pilckem Ridge, 31 July. (Q.5732)

The French had met resistance from Colonel's Farm and it was late afternoon before it fell. This forced the Scots to throw back a defensive flank to their left.

1 Guards Brigade (in support): With the 2nd Grenadier Guards on the right and the 2nd Coldstream Guards on the left, the Brigade set out at 8.50 a.m. from the Green Line. The Grenadiers came under heavy machine-gun fire from west of the Steenbeek. The situation was not helped by the 38th Division's being unable to advance at the allotted time. But, with the use of Lewis guns, the Grenadiers were able to form a defensive flank along the railway line until the 17th Royal Welsh Fusiliers (115 Brigade, 38th Division) came up. Owing to machine-gun fire from Langemarck village, the Grenadiers were forced to dig in 80 yards short of the stream. On the left, the leading company captured Signal Farm and Ruisseau Farm, crossed the Steenbeek and dug in 60 yards from the eastern bank by 9.30 a.m.

The 2nd Coldstream Guards had wheeled to the left and gained the objective. They were not able to join up with the French until late in the afternoon, after the capture of Colonel's Farm. By 10.00 a.m. the Division had captured all its objectives except on the frontage of one company on the extreme right.

British infantry cross the bridge over the canal at Boesinghe, 5 August. See also the photographs on pages 37 and 41. (Q.2681)

AUGUST

Wednesday 1 August [17]
Temperature 59°F; rain. Rainfall: 5.3mm.

15th Division (XIX Corps)
At 3.30 p.m. the Germans launched a counter-attack astride the Ypres–Roulers railway line. Under cover of smoke and an intense artillery barrage, they attacked the join between the 15th and the 8th Divisions.

North of the railway, on the 15th Division front, artillery stopped the leading waves of the German counter-attack. However, the flank of the 8/10th Gordons was exposed when the 8th Division was forced back; the left of the Gordons fell back to North Station Buildings and the right were reinforced by the 6/7th Scots Fusiliers and the 11th Argyll & Sutherland Highlanders. They were ordered to retake the Black Line and, firing as they advanced,

A 12-inch howitzer on railway mounting of the 104th Siege Battery, RGA, near Salvation Corner, just north of Ypres. The photograph is dated 3 August. (Q.7818)

drove the Germans from their gains. By 9 p.m. 45 Brigade had re-established the line prior to the German attack.

8th Division
The 8th Division was relieved by the 25th Division (II Corps).

3rd Australian Division (II ANZAC Corps)
At first light the Division spotted the Germans forming up for a counter-attack which reached the Warneton line. It was dealt with by a machine-gun barrage and artillery fire.

Thursday 2 August
Temperature 59°F; showers. Rainfall: 5.3mm.

15th Division (XIX Corps)
At 1.30 p.m., after a heavy bombardment, a German counter-attack was launched at Pommern Redoubt but was driven off. Another made at 5 p.m. was crushed by the artillery.

55th Division (XIX Corps)
At 1.30 p.m. the Germans attacked the area on and about Pommern Redoubt. This was broken up by a machine-gun and artillery fire and the attackers retired behind Hill 35.

39th Division (XVIII Corps)
The Germans were reported to be massing in front of Kitchener's Wood but were dealt with by artillery fire. 116 Brigade occupied the ruins of St Julien and posts were established on the east bank of the Steenbeek, northwards from the village.

Friday 3 August
Temperature 59°F; rain. Rainfall: 9.9mm.

30th Division (II Corps)
The 30th Division was relieved by the 18th Division (II Corps).

[17]VC: T/Capt Harold Ackroyd RAMC.

15th Division (XIX Corps)
The Division was relieved by the 16th Division (XIX Corps).

55th Division (XIX Corps)
Relieved by the 36th Division (XIX Corps).

39th Division (XVIII Corps)
A patrol of 117 Brigade penetrated as far as Maison du Rasta and Maison du Hibou.

51st Division (XVIII Corps)
Several posts were established across the Steenbeek.

Saturday 4 August
Temperature 66°F; overcast. Rainfall: 4.9mm.

41st Division (X Corps)
The Germans launched a counter-attack at Hollebeke village and Forret Farm, establishing positions there, but were later driven out.

39th Division (XVIII Corps)
Relieved by the 48th Division (XVIII Corps).

Sunday 5 August
Temperature 73°F; clear. Rainfall: nil.

19th Division (IX Corps)
The 8th North Staffs helped the 12th East Surreys (41st Division) to regain Hollebeke.

24th Division (II Corps)
The Germans attacked and captured part of Jehovah Trench.

41st Division (X Corps)
Two counter-attacks were repulsed. A third, however, again established the Germans in Hollebeke, but they were

Unloading 6-inch shells from a light railway train at Brielen on 3 August. Note the camouflage. (Q.5855)

driven out later by a counter-attack by the 12th East Surreys and the 15th Hants.

38th Division (XIV Corps)
Relieved by the 20th Division (XIV Corps).

Monday 6 August
Temperature 71F; 50% cloud cover. Rainfall: 0.1mm.

24th Division (II Corps)
The southern end of Jehovah Trench was recaptured from the Germans.

41st Division (X Corps)
The Germans launched a further counter-attack against Hollebeke but were repulsed.

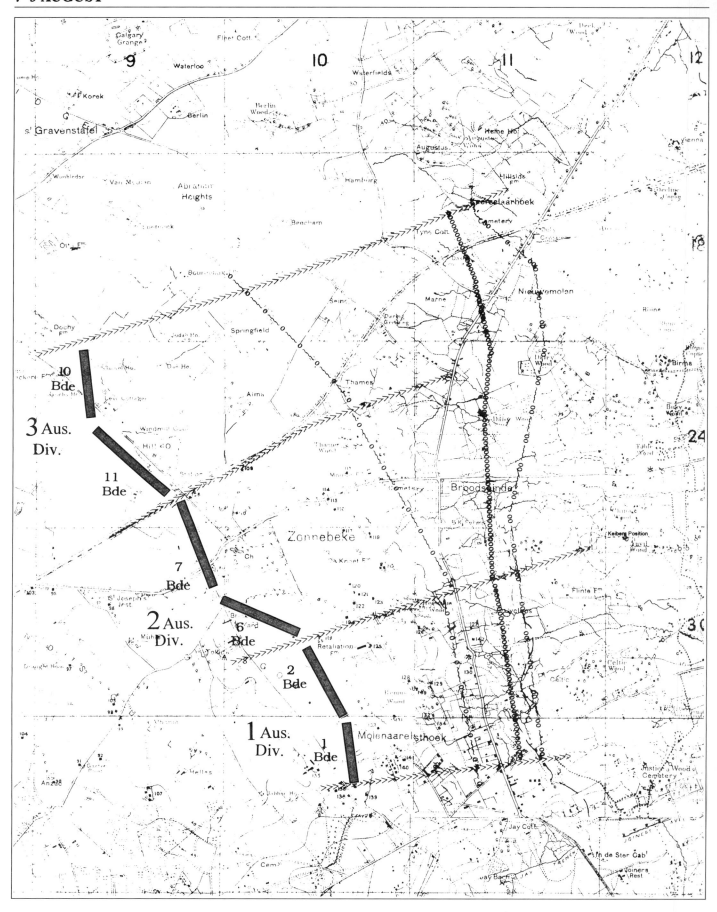

Tuesday 7 August
Temperature 69°F; cloudy. Rainfall: nil.

51st Division (XVIII Corps)
Relieved by the 11th Division (XVIII Corps).

Guards Division (XIV Corps)
Relieved by the 29th Division (XIV Corps).

20th Division (XIV Corps)
The bridge over the Steenbeek at Chien Farm was blown up by the Germans.

Wednesday 8 August
Temperature 71°F; 25% cloud cover with storms and thunder. Rainfall: 10.2mm.

37th Division (IX Corps)
111 Brigade were relieved by 12 Australian Brigade, 4th Australian Division.

19th Division (IX Corps)
The Divisional front was taken over by 112 Brigade, 37th Division.

Thursday 9 August
Temperature 68°F; clear. Rainfall: 0.2mm.

11th Division (XVIII Corps)
During the night, the Maison Bulgare and Maison du Rasta pillboxes were occupied without opposition. Posts north-east of the Steenbeek were advanced 150 yards.

Above: Men carrying 4-inch Stokes mortar bombs in canvas carriers slung on their backs, resting on light railway trucks. Brielen on 3 August. (Q.5853)

Below: The first military car to cross the new bridge at Boesinghe, 5 August. The bridge was built by Royal Engineers when the British advance had passed the canal. (Q.2680)

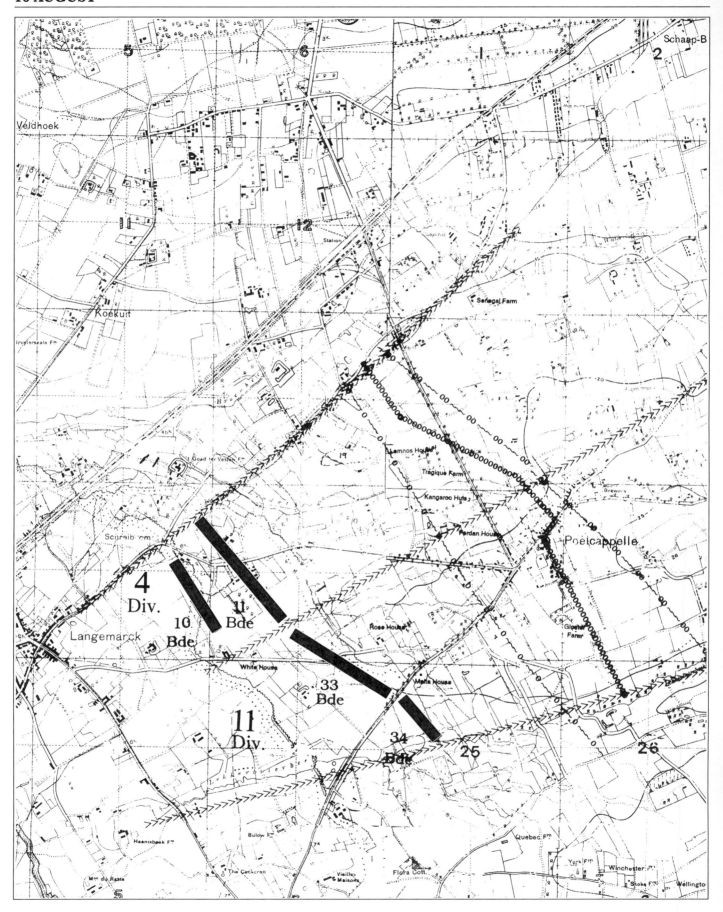

Friday 10 August

Temperature 69°F; clear . Rainfall: 1.5mm.

24th Division (II Corps)

An unsuccessful attempt was made to take Lower Star Post by the 8th Buffs (17 Brigade).

CAPTURE OF WESTHOEK

FIFTH ARMY
II Corps
18th Division

55 Brigade attacked at 4.35 a.m. with one battalion and a 46-minute barrage on a frontage of 400 yards.

The 7th Queen's were to form a defensive flank along the southern edge of Inverness Copse. At 1.30 a.m., in bright moonlight, as they moved into their assault positions, the Germans spotted them halted by a fresh line of wire posts and caused considerable losses before zero hour. The surviving Queen's moved along the eastern edge of Inverness Copse. The right com-

pany was held up by machine-gun fire from a blockhouse and a tunnel on the south-western corner of the Copse in Jasper Avenue and was pinned down. The Brigade's left flank fell back to their old front line and formed a defensive flank.

54 Brigade attacked at 4.35 a.m. with two battalions—the 11th Royal Fusiliers and the 7th Bedfords—on a frontage of 750 yards and with a 46-minute barrage.

The Fusiliers reached their objective, the Black Line, but a gap of 300 yards separated them from the Bedfords. The attack reached the German second line on either side of Fitzclarence Farm and along the sunken track at the eastern end of Glencorse Wood, but could not get in touch with 55 Brigade. At 5 p.m. the Germans started to mass for a counter-attack in Polygon and Nonne Bosschen Woods. They sent a party of bombers down Jargon Trench, and an assault from Inverness Copse under cover of a smokescreen forced the Fusiliers back

Grenadier Guardsmen outside a smashed German machine-gun emplacement at Pilckem, 5 August. (Q.2678)

to 200 yards east of Clapham Junction and the line was reinforced with all available men from HQ. This mixed unit successfully fought off two counter-attacks.

The 7th Bedfordshires caught the Germans unawares and stormed into Glencorse Wood, sending back a message to HQ at 5.13 a.m. that the wood had been taken. They tried to consolidate but, owing to marshy ground and the mud, only isolated posts were established. At 9.17 a.m. a message was sent to the effect that they still held the final objective but that the companies on the right were badly bent back. This was due to the gap between the Bedfords and the Fusiliers. Counter-attacks from Nonne Bosschen Wood were beaten off by artillery. The Germans, however, were able to push through the wood on the right, forcing back the Bedfords to Jargon Trench.

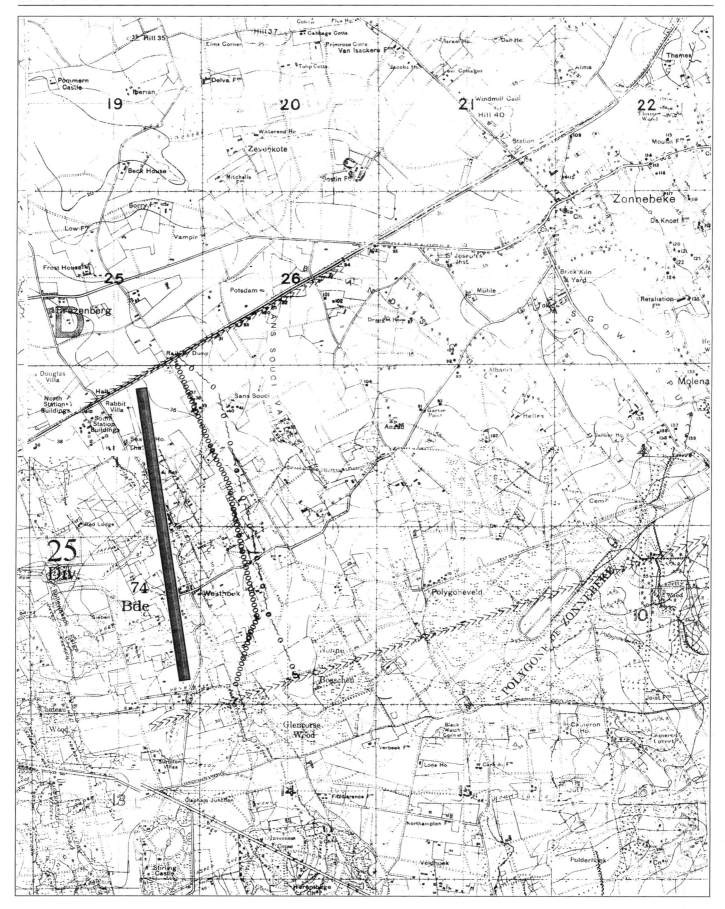

53 Brigade relieved the two assaulting brigades at 11.55 p.m. taking on the Divisional front.

25th Division

74 Brigade attacked at 4.35 a.m.with four battalions on a front of 2,000 yards after a 25-minute barrage. The attacking troops consisted of the 13th Cheshires, 2nd Royal Irish Rifles, 9th Loyal North Lancs and 11th Lancashire Fusiliers, whose left flank was on the Ypres–Roulers railway.

Left: The canal at Boesinghe after it had been passed by the British advance, showing the bridge destroyed, 6 August. (Q.2682)

Below: Artillery ammunition pack animals cross a temporary wooden bridge over the Yser Canal near Boesinghe on 9 August. Note the 18pdr round in the foreground. (Q.5863)

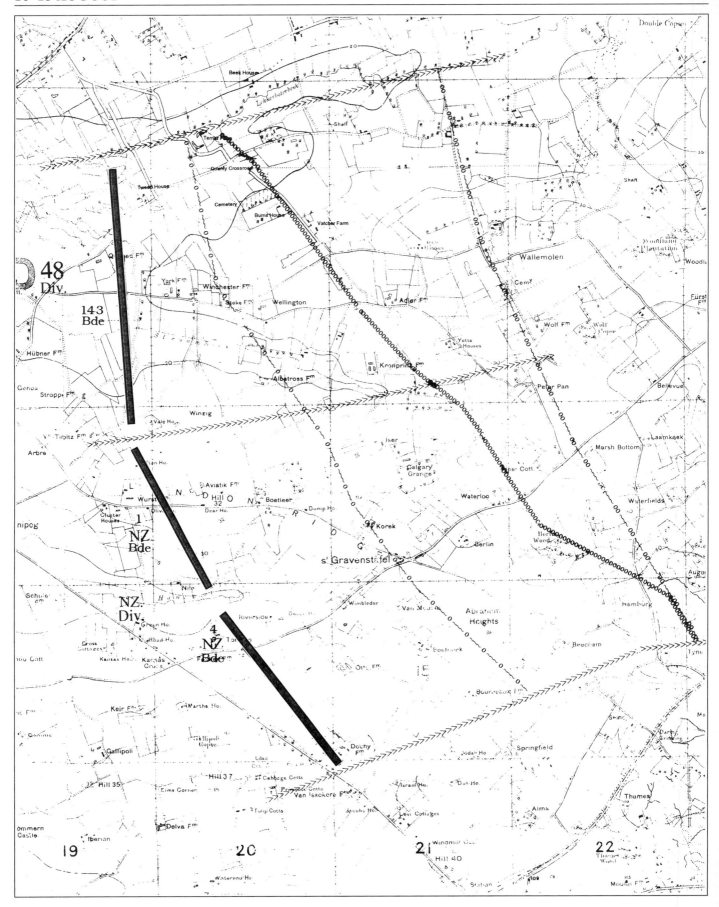

lish posts on the east bank of the Steenbeek. Passerelle Farm fell, at the second attempt, to the Middlesex. The position was consolidated and twelve double, wooden bridges were erected.

Sunday 12 August

Temperature 72°F, 75% cloud cover. Rainfall: 1.7mm.

Nothing of significance happened on this day.

Monday 13 August

Temperature 67°F; 75% cloud cover. Rainfall: nil.

18th Division (II Corps)
Relieved by the 56th Division (II Corps).

25th Division (II Corps)
Right sector relieved by the 56th Division (II Corps).

[18]VC: Pte Arnold Loosemore.

The Brigade took the outpost line and 2nd Irish Rifles rushed Westhoek village and two blockhouses. The position was protected from effective counter-attack by a stretch of deep mud in the Hanebeek valley. The mud was thirty yards wide in places and covered by over a foot of water. German artillery continued to shell the ridge and casualties were considerable. The position was consolidated.

11th Division (XVIII Corps)
The 8th Duke of Wellington's[18] (32 Brigade) attempted to advance their forward posts but met with resistance from Knoll 12 and were unsuccessful.

29th Division (XIV Corps)
At 4.15 a.m. three platoons each of the 1st Lancashire Fusiliers and the 16th Middlesex (86 Brigade) were to estab-

Saturday 11 August

Temperature 65°F; 50% cloud cover. Rainfall: 4.8mm.

18th Division (II Corps)
The Division lost a pillbox to a German attack at 4.30 a.m. during the relief of the 7th Bedfords but by 6 a.m. it had been recaptured by the 8th Norfolks.

The 7th Northamptonshire Regiment (18th Division) rest in camp near Dickebusch after the attack in Shrewsbury Forest on 31 July in which they lost their CO, eleven officers and 246 men. The photograph is dated 9 August. (Q.5847)

Above, far left: : Ruins in Wytschaete, 11 August. A dud 30cm shell lies in the foreground. (Q.5868)

Left: Carrying up sleepers for a light railway at Wytschaete, 11 August 1917. The uncompleted track can be seen. (Q.5872)

Above, centre: A corporal checks 8-inch shells arriving on a light railway at Wytschaete, 11 August. (Q.5871)

Above right: Two officers utilize the bonnet and front wheels of a destroyed lorry as a seat while looking at the map. Near St Eloi, 11 August. (Q.5877)

20th Division (XIV Corps)

The Division made another attempt to gain ground with 59 Brigade and the 6th Yorks (11th Division), with some limited success.

Tuesday 14 August

Temperature 79°F; rain. Rainfall: 18.1mm.

25th Division (II Corps)

The left sector of the 25th Division (II Corps) was relieved by the 8th Division (II Corps).

20th Division (XIV Corps)

Attacking at 4 a.m. with the 10th and 11th Rifle Brigades across the Steenbeek, the Division was able to establish a line on the east bank. The crossing of the stream was made easier by bridges brought up by the assaulting troops. The 10th RB were held up by fire from Au Bon Gite, but they managed to take Mill Mound and four small concrete bunkers. Despite surrounding the main building, they had to settle for digging-in 20 yards west of Au Bon Gite. The 11th RB moved forward and consolidation was under way by 6 a.m.

Wednesday 15 August

Temperature 65°F; overcast. Rainfall: 7.8mm.

41st Division (X Corps)

Relieved by the 39th Division (XVIII Corps).

20th Division (XIV Corps)

The Germans counter-attacked the 11th Rifle Brigade (59 Brigade) but were repulsed at 5 a.m.

Thursday 16 August

Temperature 68°F; overcast. Rainfall: nil.

BATTLE OF LANGEMARCK (16–18 August)

FIFTH ARMY
II Corps
56th Division

The Division attacked at 4.45 a.m. with two brigades, plus one from the 18th Division.

53 Brigade (18th Division) was used to form a defensive flank from the eastern corner of Stirling Castle to Black Watch Corner.

The 7th Bedfords (54th Brigade, 18th Division), attacking the north-west corner of Inverness Copse, were

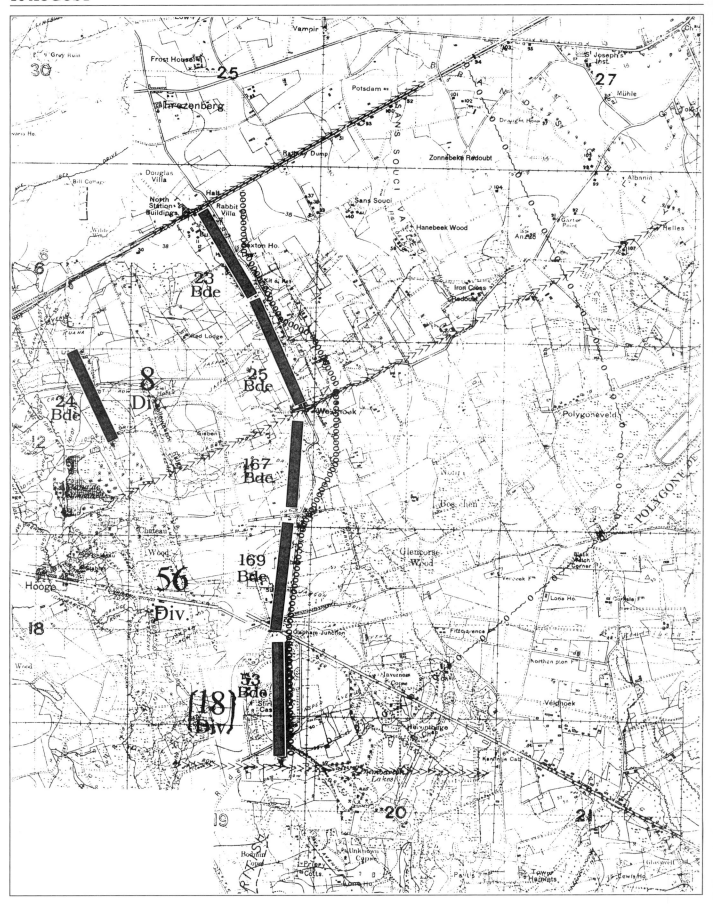

stopped at once by a blockhouse on the north-west of the copse. The 4th London Regiment (attached from 56th Division) were brought to a standstill to the north of the western side of the copse and eventually established a defensive flank along the southern edge of Glencorse Wood.

169 Brigade: The 5th and 2nd London Regiments encountered a marsh in their advance. The 2nd London edged to the right, pushing the 5th still further right and causing a large gap to develop between this and 53 Brigade. Beyond the marsh, in the middle of Glencorse Wood, was a sunken lane lined with pillboxes. This caused some delay but the wood was eventually cleared. It was believed that the leading waves entered Polygon Wood; the second wave, though, was checked by fire from Polygon Wood and was forced back until the 9th London, in support, were brought up. Later in the day a German counter-attack from the east and south drove the whole Brigade back to its starting trenches.

167 Brigade: The 8th Middlesex and the 1st London Regiment encountered a marsh and were forced to the left to avoid it. The 8th Middlesex found another lake of mud four feet deep at the northern end of Nonne Bosschen. Their right flank was exposed and the 1st London came under heavy shelling, which, delaying them, caused the waves to become mixed up. This meant that the ground over which the advance had been made was not properly cleared and pockets of Germans remained behind them. It was believed that some of the attacking troops reached north of Polygon Wood, but these were never seen again.

At 3 p.m. the enemy were seen massing opposite the 25th Brigade (8th Division) and on the left of the 56th Division, but they were dispersed by artillery fire. At about 5 p.m. the Brigade retired to a position which gave them a gain of 400 yards.

German prisoners captured in the Battle of Ypres. Near Proven, 16 August. (Q.2720)

8th Division

The Division attacked at 4.45 a.m. with two brigades, plus one in support.

25 Brigade: The 2nd Royal Berkshires had their right on the Westhoek–Zonnebeke road in touch with the 56th Division. On their left were the 1st Royal Irish Rifles, and the 2nd Lincolns were in support. The Berks advanced across the Hanebeek, and it became clear that the 56th Division would not be up to form a flank, so a company was detailed to do so. Although receiving machine-gun fire from Nonne Bosschen and Polygon Wood, they managed to secure most of Iron Cross Redoubt. Later in the day they came under fire from two directions.

The Irish Rifles and the 2nd West Yorks (23 Brigade), in the centre of the Brigade, were not affected as much by the hold-ups on the flanks. They passed through Hanebeek Wood and continued up the ridge. Anzac and Zonnebeke Redoubts were also captured and the final objective was occupied at 7 a.m., whence began consolidation. A number of German counter-attacks were repulsed.

At this stage the 8th Division was 1,000 yards ahead of the other two divisions (56th and 16th) on its flanks,

leaving it exposed to a number of enemy counter-attacks, and the position became untenable. At 9 a.m. the Irish were forced back to the road west of Anzac which fell to the Germans, leaving the Berks in a very exposed position.

At about 10.15 a.m. the Brigade was forced to retire to west of the Hanebeek; this in turn forced 23 Brigade to fall back. Later in the evening it was decided not to hold this exposed position and the Division retired to the original Black Line 200 yards from its starting place.

23 Brigade: The 2nd West Yorkshire Regiment and the 2nd Middlesex—which had its left flank on Ypres–Roulers railway—were to assault, with the 2nd Scottish Rifles in support. At first all went well, but at 5.05 a.m. the Middlesex, who had overtaken the 16th Division on their left flank, came under fire from the railway embankment and Potsdam Redoubt in the 16th Division's area. They formed a front facing north with their right on the enclosure north of Sans Souci.

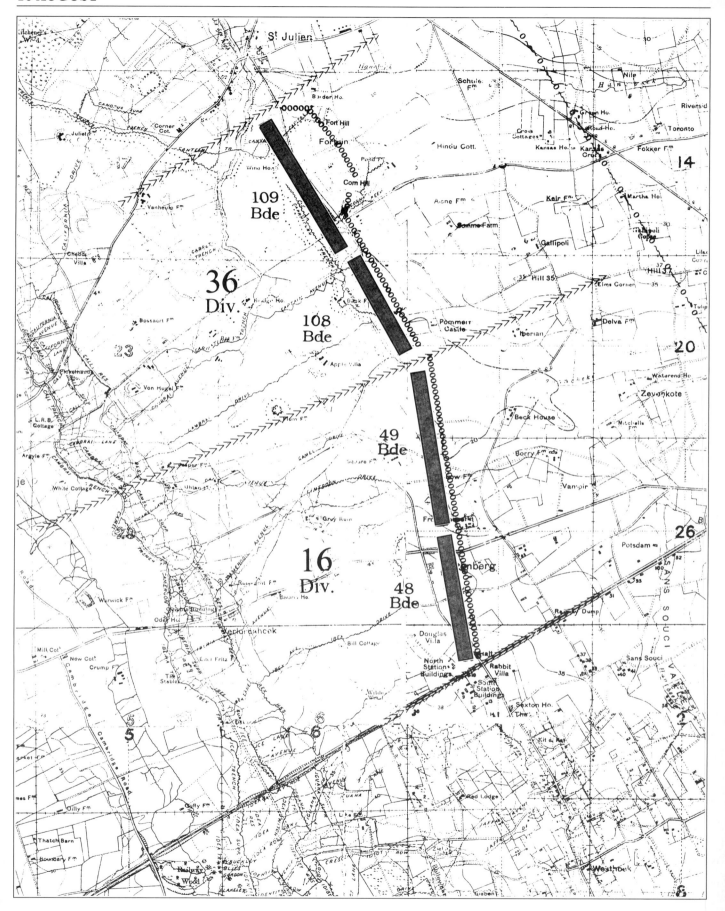

The West Yorks kept pace with the Middlesex and by 7.30 a.m. an outpost line was established on the eastern slope of Westhoek Ridge. At 9.30 a.m. a German counter-attack forced the British back to Hanebeek Wood. At 3.30 p.m. another counter-attack was launched in which the enemy almost reached the wood.

24 Brigade were to take over the defence of the ridge after the attacking battalions had advanced.

XIX Corps
16th Division
The Division attacked at 4.45 a.m., zero hour, with two brigades.

48 Brigade attacked with the 7th Royal Irish Rifles on the left and the 9th Royal Dublin Fusiliers on the right; the

A shell bursting near an 8-inch howitzer battery near Boesinghe during the Battle of Langemarck, 17 August. Three men may be seen behind tree trunks, sheltering from shell splinters. (Q.5889)

2nd and 8th Royal Dublin Fusiliers (combined) were in support, with the 1st Royal Munster Fusiliers (47 Brigade) in reserve. The assault troops attacked Vampir Farm and Potsdam and dug in just in front of these positions. At 9 a.m. the 2nd Royal Dublin Fusiliers moved up in support of the 9th Dublins and got to within 100 yards of Bit Work, east of Vampir (which they held until withdrawing at 10 p.m.).

At 3.30 p.m. the enemy counter-attacked and, as the Division had both flanks in the air, it was forced to fall back to its old front line.

49 Brigade[19] attacked with the 8th Inniskilling Fusiliers on the right and the 7th Inniskilling Fusiliers on the left; the 7th/8th Royal Irish Fusiliers were in support, with the 6th Royal Irish Regiment (47 Brigade) in reserve. Keeping close to the barrage, they managed to capture the Green Line and a strongpoint called Beck House within an hour. The advance continued with the

7th Inniskillings towards Delva Farm; they took it before coming under fire from pillboxes in their rear which they had failed to mop up. The 8th Inniskillings, advancing towards Borry Farm, were held up by machine-gun fire.

36th Division
The Division attacked with two brigades.

108 Brigade attacked with the 9th Royal Irish Fusiliers and the 13th Royal Irish Rifles; the 12th Royal Irish Rifles were in support and the 11th Royal Irish Rifles were in reserve. The assaulting troops came under heavy fire from the blockhouses, including Somme, on their front. Some troops were observed attacking Gallipoli on the right and a few were seen on the Green Line, but both these positions were impossible to hold. By 10 a.m. the Brigade was back at its starting point.

[19]VC: A/L-Cpl Frederick George Room.

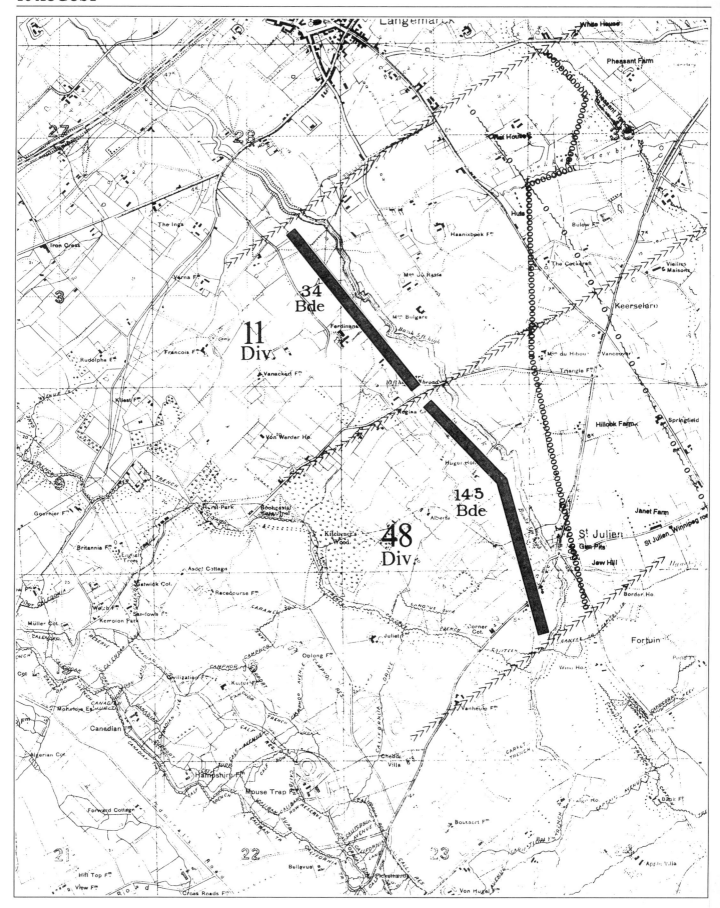

109 *Brigade* attacked with the 14th Royal Irish Rifles and the 11th Royal Inniskilling Fusiliers; the 9th Inniskilling Fusiliers were in support and the 10th in reserve. The Brigade experienced difficulties similar to those of the 108th Brigade but managed to take Fort Hill≈Corn Hill and dug in. No further attacks were launched that day.

XVIII Corps
48th Division

The Division attacked at 4.45 a.m., zero hour, with one brigade.

145 Brigade attacked with the 1/5th Gloucesters, 1/1st and 1/4th Ox & Bucks Light Infantry, with the 1/4th Royal Berks in reserve. The Gloucesters took Border House and Gun Pits on the north and south of the St Julien–Winnepeg road and were held up by machine-gun fire from Janet Farm. A small counter-attack was launched by the Germans but was broken up by small-arms fire. The 1/5th Gloucesters fought hard to take the last house in St Julien then carried on the advance, digging in on a line of Border House–Jew Hill–Gun Pits–St Julien. They came under cross-fire from Hillock Farm and Maison du Hibou but the former fell to the 1/1st Ox & Bucks Light Infantry. When the Brigade topped the rise 200 yards east of the Steenbeek a few Bucks were seen to reach Springfield Farm near the objective, but they were never seen again.

At 7 a.m. Battalion Headquarters was established in a blockhouse on the west side of the Hillock Farm–St Julien road. The 1/4th Royal Berks were brought up as a left flank guard. At 9 a.m. the Germans started to gather around Triangle Farm and at 10 a.m. a strong counter-attack was fought off.

Dusk came at 7.30 p.m. when around 100 Germans attempted to rush the

gun pits on the left but were forced off. At 9.30 p.m. a counter-attack from Triangle Farm was launched with little success.

11th Division

The Division attacked at 4.45 a.m., zero hour, with one brigade.

34 Brigade: The 8th Northumberland Fusiliers and the 5th Dorset Regiment were the initial assault troops for the Brigade. The attack was then taken over by the 11th Manchester Regiment and the 9th Lancashire Fusiliers, with the 7th South Staffs and the 9th Sherwood Foresters (both 33 Brigade).

The right flank was exposed to machine-gun fire owing to 145 Brigade (48th Division) being held up. The 8th Northumberland Fusiliers in their turn were held up by isolated posts and blockhouses, with the result that the

A Royal Engineer establishes communication by means of a Fuller phone at an old German concrete emplacement near Zuydschoote, 17 August. (Q.2730)

A mounted British gunner receives a glass of water from a French girl near Watou, 17 August. (Q.2728)

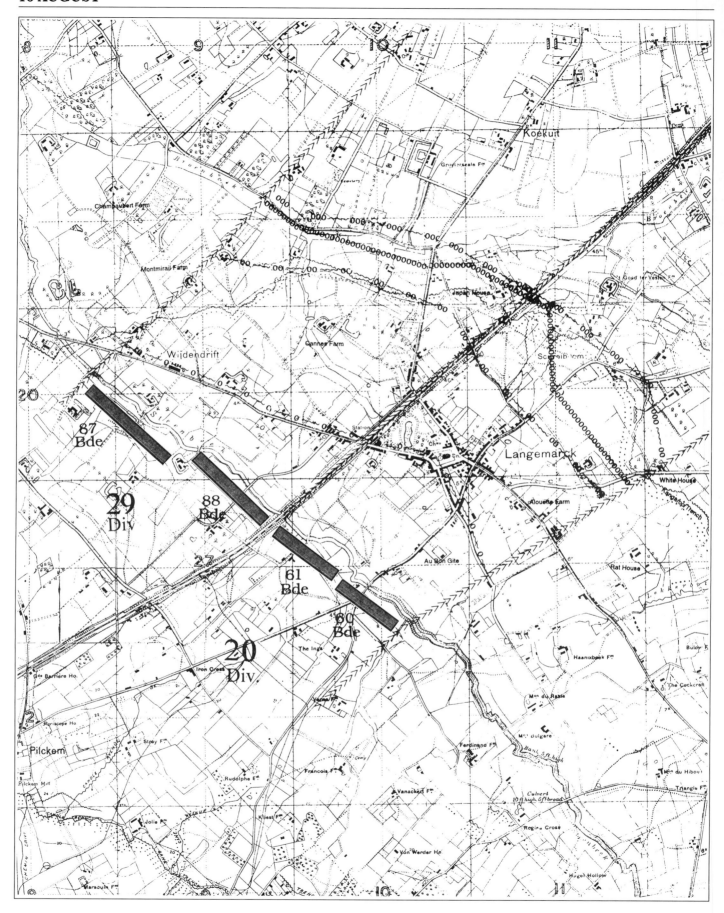

barrage got away from them. However, the left pushed on and dug in 100 yards west of Langemarck Road with its left on the cemetery, although the exposed right flank, under heavy fire from Maison du Hibou and the Triangle, dug in facing east.

The 11th Manchesters, due to take over the attack, suffered heavily from fire on their way up to the Northumberland Fusiliers. After crossing the Steenbeek they came under heavy fire from Maison du Hibou and the Triangle. On reaching Cockcroft it was found to be unoccupied and they passed through it. Still under fire from Maison du Hibou (not taken by 145 Brigade, 48th Division), a defensive flank was formed. The remainder of the Battalion came under fire from Bulow Farm. The leading companies fell back to some huts, joined up with the 9th Lancashire Fusiliers and consolidated the position.

The 5th Dorsets advanced steadily, in touch with 61 Brigade on the left (20th Division), but were unable to link with the 8th Northumberlands. The Langemarck Road was reached and consolidation was started. The right made a defensive flank to the south side of Haanixbeek Farm. The 9th Lancs went well until coming under fire from Bulow Farm on the right and from a work on their front. They held for a while and then fell back in line with the 11th Manchester Regiment.

The left company, going from Rat House to Pheasant Trench, captured their objective, while the right became a little disorganized and separated from the left. However, part of Pheasant Trench was blocked and consolidated. A platoon was detailed to take White House, which it did, but came under heavy shell-fire. It was agreed with the 6th King's Shropshire Light Infantry (60th Brigade, 20th Division) to with-

The Battle of Langemarck: a distant shell-burst seen from near Pilckem, 17 August. A German machine-gun emplacement is visible in the foreground. (Q.2707)

draw to 50 yards west of White House. At the end of the day the position was a line running from Pheasant Trench west of Rat House and joining up with the 11th Manchesters on the Lekkerboterbeek.

XIV Corps
20th Division

The Division attacked at 4.45 a.m., zero hour, with two brigades.

60 Brigade attacked initially on a one-battalion front with the 6th Ox & Bucks Light Infantry, with the 6th King's Shropshire Light Infantry and the 12th King's Royal Rifle Corps[20] to come through and take the third objective.

---

[20]VC: Sgt Edward Cooper.

This left the 12th Rifle Brigade in reserve.

After crossing the Steenbeek, movement was restricted to small columns of men in single file which wound their way between craters full of water or mud. Alouette Farm fell to the 6th KSLI and the first objective was gained with little trouble.

The Brigade formed up east of the second objective, having cleared Langemarck, ready to assault the final objective. At 7.20 a.m. they advanced. The KSLI, on the right, when 100 yards east of Alouette Farm, came under heavy fire from Rat House and White House, the latter eventually being captured by them. By 7.45 a.m. the final objective had been taken and held. The Germans forced out of Kangaroo Trench made for a small wood behind White House.

The line was held by the 6th KSLI (whose right flank was on the second objective, Rat House still being under enemy control), the 12th KRRC, the 12th King's Liverpool Regiment and the 7th DCLI (the last two 61 Brigade). The position was consolidated in time to repel the first of the counter-attacks.

At around 4 p.m. the enemy crept up and attacked at the junction of 60 and 61 Brigades around Schreiboom and the 12th KRRC and the 12th King's were driven back some 200 yards. The KSLI lent a platoon, four Lewis guns, two Vickers guns and fifteen boxes of small-arms ammunition to the KRRC to help out and they drove the enemy out of the Cemetery. *61 Brigade* advanced on a two-battalion front, with the 7th King's Own Yorkshire Light Infantry[21] and the 7th Somerset Light Infantry to attack the first two objectives and the 12th King's and the 7th Duke of Cornwall's Light Infantry to attack the third.

The Brigade came under enfilade fire from Au Bon Gite until it fell to the 11th Rifle Brigade (59 Brigade). The advance continued until it came under

fire from a blockhouse west of Lange-marck and later at Langemarck Station. Once the station and railway trucks had fallen, comparatively little opposition was met.

At 7.20 a.m. the whole line advanced to the final objective, though it met with strong opposition from concealed

Left: An old German pillbox shelter, showing a machine-gun emplacement, at the top of Hill 60, 17 August. Note the steel in the concrete construction. (E[AUS].584)

Below: Vehicles of many kinds wait at Dickebusch in order to load up petrol cans filled with water, 18 August. (Q.5886)

parties of Germans. By 7.45 a.m. the third objective was in the hands of the 20th Division, although Rat House, south-east of Langemarck, had not fallen.

29th Division

The Division attacked at 4.45 a.m., zero hour, with two brigades.

88 Brigade attacked with the 2nd Hampshires and the Newfoundland Regiment, with the 1st Essex in support. They took their first objective and the Hants assisted 61 Brigade (20th Division) on their right in taking the Blue Line. The Newfoundlanders took over the attack. In very marshy conditions

they came under fire from Cannes Farm; this was cleared and they went on to take the Green Line and consolidate. Continuing, they took the Red Line and sent out patrols to take Japan House in front of it. This they accomplished.

87 Brigade consisted of the 1st King's Own Scottish Borderers[22] and the 2nd South Wales Borderers, with the 1st Border Regiment in support. The first objective fell with little trouble, but on the way to the second they were held up by fire from Champaubert Farm blockhouse in the French sector and also from Montmirail Farm. The French brought down a barrage, enabling the South Wales Borderers to take Montmirail Farm. They then pushed on to the final objective, which was consolidated at around 10 a.m. Patrols were pushed out in the direction of the Broembeek. At 4 p.m. the Germans launched a counter-attack, which was dealt with by artillery and small-arms fire.

Friday 17 August

Temperature 72°F; clear. Rainfall: nil.

48th Division (XVIII Corps)

At 2.30 a.m. a company of Worcesters unsuccessfully attacked Maison du Hibou.

16th Division (XIX Corps)

Relieved by the 15th Division (XIX Corps).

36th Division (XIX Corps)

Relieved by the 61st Division (XIX Corps).

20th Division (XIV Corps)

Relieved by the 38th Division (XIV Corps).

[21]VC: Pte Wilfred Edwards.
[22]VC: A/Coy QMS William Henry Grimbaldeston.

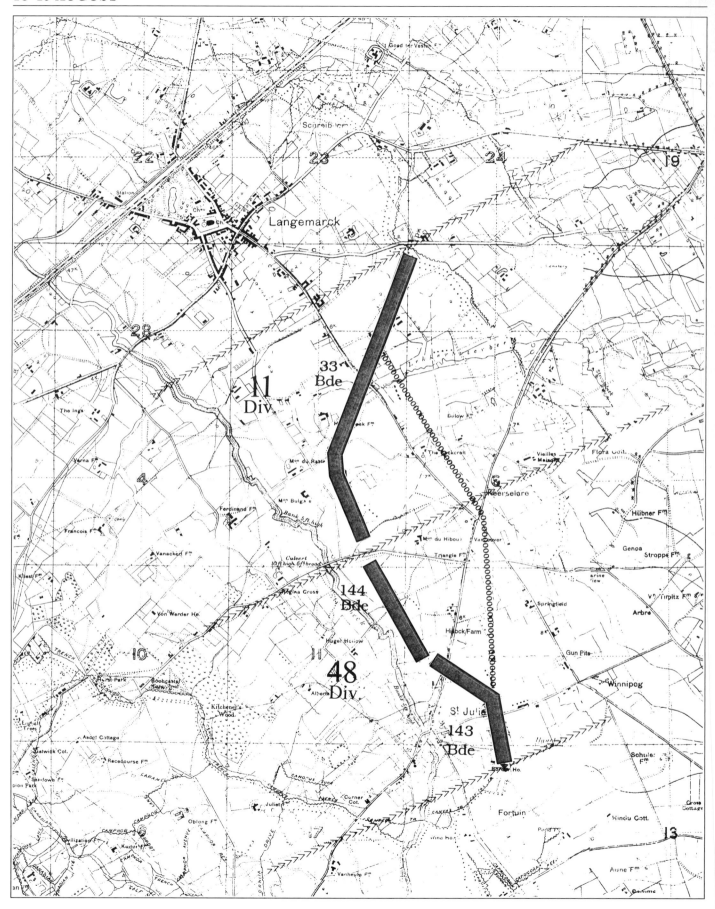

Saturday 18 August

Temperature 74°F; clear. Rainfall: nil.

56th Division (II Corps)
Relieved by the 14th Division (II Corps).

14th Division
43 Brigade attacked with the 6th Somerset Light Infantry and the 6th Duke of Cornwall's Light Infantry. The Somersets advanced through Inverness Copse following the barrage. The Cornwalls, crossing the plateau, were soon held up by machine-gun fire from Fitzclarence Farm and an L-shaped farm 200 yards north of it. They were counter-attacked and forced to fall back to half way through the copse, but, with the help of two tanks coming along the Menin Road, they held on and were supported during the day. They sustained another three German counter-attacks through the afternoon.

29th Division[23]
Posts were established east of the Broembeek.

Sunday 19 August

Temperature 69°F; 50% cloud cover. Rainfall: nil.

8th Division (II Corps)
Relieved by the 47th Division (X Corps).

48th Division (XVIII Corps)
At 4.45 a.m., seven tanks of 1 Tank Brigade, with companies of the 1/8th Worcestershire Regiment in support, moved along the St Julien–Poelcapelle road under cover of a smoke and shrapnel barrage and captured four pillboxes which had held up the Division on the 16th. Their fate was as follows: Hillock Farm fell at 6 a.m. when the garrison ran away; at Maison du Hibou,

A 9.2-inch howitzer and its team at St Jean, in a photograph dated 19 August. (Q.5997)

the tanks could get no closer than 80 yards away because of boggy ground (the male tank stood off and fired 50 shells from the rear, forcing the garrison to run and be shot down by a female tank working in close co-operation); Triangle Farm was kept under covering fire as the infantry entered and killed the garrison; and the Cockcroft, which fell at 6.45 a.m., was harassed by a female tank which ditched 50 yards away (as many as one hundred Germans ran away from this pillbox and the surrounding bunkers and the majority of them were shot down). The strongpoint was occupied and all seven tanks managed to return from the action.[24]

---

[23]VC: A/Coy Sgt-Maj John Skinner.
[24]This was the first definite success gained through the use of tanks in the 1917 offensives.

Monday 20 August

Temperature 71°F; 50% cloud cover. Rainfall: nil.

24th Division (II Corps)
No 2 Special Company Royal Engineers discharged gas and smoke bombs on Jehu Trench and strongpoint, east of Lower Star Post.

61st Division (XIX Corps)
A platoon from the 2/8th Worcesters (182 Brigade) overran a German outpost near Somme Farm.

Tuesday 21 August

Temperature 72°F; clear. Rainfall: nil.

38th Division (XIV Corps)
The Division advanced the left of their line.

Wednesday 22 August

Temperature 78°F; 50% cloud cover. Rainfall: nil.

24th Division (II Corps)
The 1st Royal Fusiliers (17 Brigade) attacked and took a strongpoint from their position near Bodmin Copse.

47th Division (X Corps)
The Division assisted the 15th Division in their attack by sending out patrols.

15th Division (XIX Corps)
The Division attacked at 4.45 a.m. with two brigades.
45 Brigade attacked with the 13th Royal Scots and the 11th Argyll & Sutherland Highlanders. They reached Potsdam, Vampir and Borry Farms as flares showed. Machine guns accounted for most of the attacking infantry, while

the survivors of both battalions fell back to establish a line from Railway Dump along the road to Beck House. *44 Brigade* attacked with the 8th Seaforths and the 7th Camerons. Both suffered heavily from machine-gun fire and made little headway. The Camerons and a party of the 9th Gordons[25] gained a footing on Hill 35. During the rest of the day the 13th Royal Scots (45 Brigade) tried repeatedly to get forward, but they were unsuccessful.

Between 1 and 3 p.m. two weak counter-attacks were launched and both were dealt with by artillery and rifle fire.

61st Division (XIX Corps)
The Division attacked with one brigade.
184 Brigade attacked with the 2/1st and 2/4th Ox & Bucks Light Infantry, with the 2/5th Gloucestershire Regiment in support. Both battalions went well

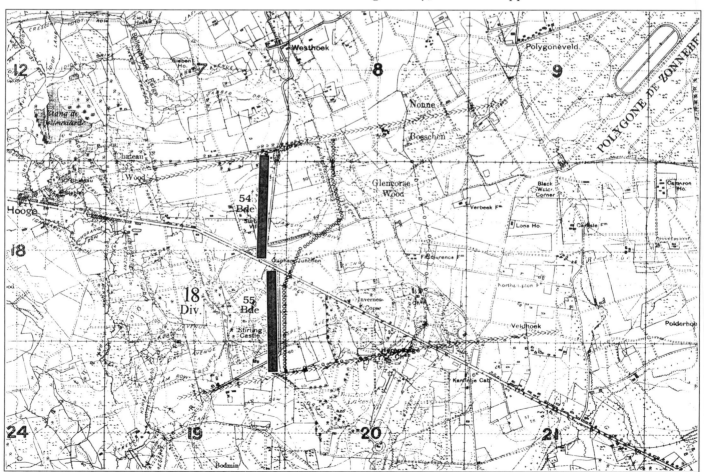

and 30 minutes after the start were digging-in 150 yards west of the Winnipeg–Kansas crossroads. After consolidation, they came under fire from Schuler Galleries. The right, however, was held up by Pond Farm. At noon two platoons unsuccessfully attacked it, but it later fell to the Gloucesters after heavy fighting, as did Hindu Cottage.

48th Division (XVIII Corps)

The Division attacked with two brigades.

143 Brigade: At 4.45 a.m. the 1/5th Royal Warwicks attacked Springfield and Winnipeg and 'C' Company succeeded in capturing the gunpits. The conditions prevented further waves

Infantry wearing bandoliers of ammunition in support trenches at Wieltje, 19 August 1917. Note the bayonets tied to the stocks. (Q.5888)

going forward, however, and the gunpits fell to a counter-attack, though they were recaptured later that day.

144 Brigade: The 1/6th Gloucesters attacked at 4.45 a.m. At 6.30 a.m. they were reported to be within 50 yards of Springfield Road and in touch with the Warwicks of 143 Brigade. Tanks, which could not leave the road owing to the mud, were said to be dealing with Vancouver. At 8.15 a.m. it was reported that the pillbox had been captured but lost again because of a counter-attack made from an old gunpit to the right. The Brigade position was now midway between Springfield Road and the original position. That night, posts were established on the road.

11th Division (XVIII Corps)

The Division attacked with one brigade (the 33rd), aided by two tanks, *Dracula* (male) and *Devil* (female). The tanks advanced with the infantry but,

on reaching the St Julien–Langemarck crossroads, encountered fallen trees blocking the road 150 yards from the objective. Unable to proceed any further, they opened fire on Vieilles Maisons, which they were opposite at the time, and started for home. *Devil* received a direct hit, killing two crew members. *Dracula* was not seen again until the evening, when it was located on the west side of the Poelcappelle road.

The 6th Lincolns, advancing as close to the barrage as possible, took Bulow Farm and dug in. As the 48th Division on their right was held up, they had to form a defensive flank.

The 6th Borderers advanced at zero hour and met with little resistance. They took their objective without delay and consolidated their position.

[25]The Gordons were in an attack for the first time since the Battle of Loos in 1915.

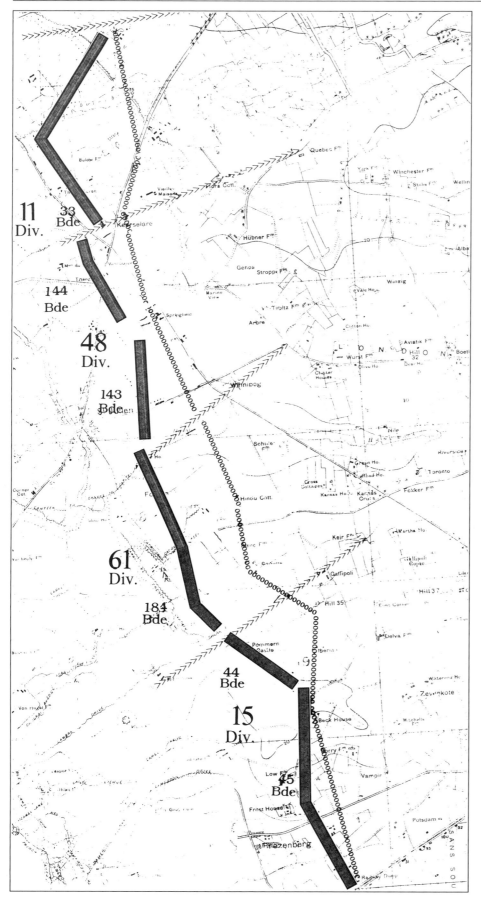

Thursday 23 August

Temperature 74°F; 50% cloud cover. Rainfall: 1.4mm.

15th Division (XIX Corps)

44 Brigade attacked Gallipoli with the 9th Black Watch and the 8/10th Gordons while the 8th Seaforths attacked Iberian Farm. Neither attack was successful, though the Black Watch advanced their line 80 yards.

Friday 24 August

Temperature 68°F; 50% cloud cover. Rainfall: 0.1mm.

14th Division (II Corps)

At 4 a.m. a heavy German barrage fell on Inverness Copse and north as far as Glencorse Wood. At 4.30 a.m. the German infantry attacked; south of Glencorse Wood the attack was with bombers and flame-throwers. The forward posts were held by companies of the 6th King's Own Yorkshire Light Infantry, which were forced back, as were the 6th Cornwalls to their start line of the 22nd.

At Inverness Copse the German attack was not as effective. At 12.45 p.m. the defenders, the 10th DLI, fell back to the west. That evening, when relieved, they were holding the western edge of the copse to the Menin Road, to a point where Jargon Drive cut the sunken road north of the Menin Road.

61st Division (XIX Corps)

The Division attacked in the evening. A platoon of the 2/7th Worcesters (182 Brigade) attempted to outflank Aisne Farm but was stopped by machine-gun fire.

48th Division (XVIII Corps)

The gunpits around Springfield were counter-attacked with flame-throwers, but the Germans were driven off.

Saturday 25 August

Temperature 67°F; 50% cloud cover. Rainfall: nil.

14th Division (II Corps)

The Division was relieved by the 23rd Division (X Corps).

15th Division (XIX Corps)

Another attempt to take Gallipoli was made by two companies of the 9th Black Watch (44 Brigade). Although unsuccessful, they managed to gain 170 yards, which they consolidated. The 10th Scottish Rifles attempted unsuccessfully to take Iberian Farm.

61st Division (XIX Corps)

At 11 p.m. another unsuccessful assault was made on Aisne Farm by the 2/7th Worcesters.

48th Division (XVIII Corps)

The Division, with 143 Brigade, attacked and captured some gunpits.

Sunday 26 August

Temperature 70°F; overcast. Rainfall: 19.6mm.

24th Division (II Corps)

The Germans rushed and captured an outpost. It was, however, immediately recaptured and the line re-established.

23rd Division (X Corps)

At dawn the enemy attacked four posts with flame-throwers, forcing one post back.

Right, upper: A 6-inch, 26 cwt howitzer ready for firing at Pilckem, 23 August 1917. (Q.2751)

Right, lower: A doctor attends to a man wounded in the shoulder at a captured German dump at Oosttaverne on 25 August. Note the camouflage screen and the 76mm Minenwerfer ammunition. (Q.5916)

61st Division (XIX Corps)

The Division attacked Schuler Galleries, without success.

Monday 27 August

Temperature 57°F; 50% cloud cover. Rainfall: 15.3mm.

8th Division (II Corps)

The Division entered the line.

23rd Division (X Corps)

41 Brigade: At daybreak the Brigade, with two tanks in support, unsuccessfully attacked 600 yards of trench running from the Menin Road and through the western edge of Inverness Copse.

61st Division (XIX Corps)

183 Brigade attacked the Schuler Farm–Gallipoli line with the 2/4th Gloucesters and the 2/8th Warwicks but was unsuccessful.

15th Division (XIX Corps)

46 Brigade: A further attempt was made to take Gallipoli Farm, this time by the 10/11th Highland Light Infantry. They reached the farm buildings but were forced back by enemy machine-gun fire.

48th Division (XVIII Corps)

144 Brigade attacked at 1.55 p.m. with the 1/8th and 1/7th Worcestershire Regiment. They were forced to clear the occupied shell holes, and at least

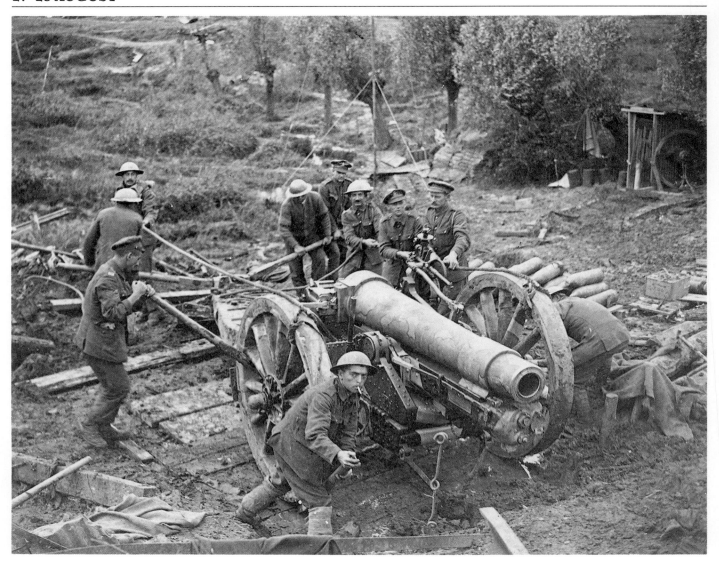

RFA personnel manhandle a 6-inch, 26 cwt howitzer at Ypres, 27 August. (Q.5945)

one concrete bunker, as they went. They came under enfilade fire from Springfield Farm on the right of the attack; in the centre, Vancouver Farm gave similar trouble. As darkness fell, Springfield Farm succumbed to the 1/8th; it was outflanked and taken from the north.

145 Brigade supported the attack of 144 Brigade with the 1/4th Royal Berks and the 1/4th Ox & Bucks Light Infantry but also came under fire from Springfield Farm. The Ox & Bucks relieved the Worcesters (144 Brigade) at midnight.

Neither brigade had made much headway owing to the knee-deep mud, and both dug in as best as they could.

11th Division (XVIII Corps)
32 Brigade: The advance started well for the 9th West Yorks but soon came under fire from Pheasant Trench and Vancouver. However, they pressed on. The right came under fire from Vieilles Maisons and they seized the nearest concrete building. Two platoons from the 6th Yorks & Lancs were sent up to reinforce.

It was a similar story for the 8th Duke of Wellington's. They came under fire from a machine gun on the roof of Pheasant Farm and the right of the Battalion dug in 60 yards from its origi-

nal position. The left, however, reached Pheasant Trench and occupied part of it. The 6th Yorkshire Regiment were sent up to help fill the line.

38th Division (XIV Corps)
The Division attacked at 1.55 p.m., lost the barrage almost immediately and then, caught by fire from Pheasant Farm, was forced back to its start line.

Tuesday 28 August
Temperature 62°F; 50% cloud cover. Rainfall: 0.9mm

15th Division (XIX Corps)
Relieved by the 42nd Division (XV Corps).

11th Division (XVIII Corps)

The Germans holding Vieilles Maisons withdrew during the night and the position was occupied by the 6th Yorks & Lancs (32nd Brigade).

An informal truce now commenced along the battle front, with both sides sending out stretcher-bearers to search the many shell holes and bring in the wounded, irrespective of nationality.

Wednesday 29 August

Temperature 61°F; 50% cloud cover. Rainfall: 2.6mm.

11th Division (XVIII Corps)

Relieved by the 58th Division.

29th Division (XIV Corps)

The 29th Division was relieved by the Guards Division (XIV Corps).

Thursday 30 August

Temperature 63°F; 50% cloud cover. Rainfall: 0.7mm.

38th Division (XIV Corps)

The White House was entered by patrols.

25th Division (II Corps)

7 Brigade took over the Glencorse Wood sector under the command of the 23rd Division (X Corps).

The effect of a British 9.2-inch shell on a reinforced concrete German dug-out located near Hill 60, 27 August. The dug-out was sited some 10 feet below ground level and the concrete roof and walls were over two feet thick. (E[AUS].665)

Friday 31 August

Temperature 64°F; 50% cloud cover. Rainfall: 0.7mm.

61st Division (XIX Corps)

182 Brigade completed the relief of the 15th Division, which had been started on 28 August by the 42nd Division (XV Corps), including Gallipoli and Hill 35.

A view of the ruins of Poelcappelle.
The blockhouse on the right has been
destroyed by gunfire; the left-hand one
has been evacuated. The photograph
was taken under German observation,
13 September. (Q.3029)

SEPTEMBER

Saturday 1 September

Temperature 59°F; 50% cloud cover. Rainfall: 0.2mm.

24th Division (II Corps)
The enemy attacked Inverness Copse, but were beaten off after heavy fighting.

61st Division (XIX Corps)
182 Brigade: An attempt was made by the 2/5th Warwicks to rush the enemy position on Hill 35. They managed to occupy a small portion.

Sunday 2 September

Temperature 63°F; overcast. Rainfall: 1.1mm.

47th Division (X Corps)
The Division was relieved by the 25th Division (II Corps) and 42nd Division (XV Corps).

Ruins in the village of Passchendaele. (Q.45460)

Monday 3 September

Temperature 69°F; clear. Rainfall: nil.

30th Division (II Corps)
Relieved by the 14th Division (X Corps).

61st Division (XIX Corps)
182 Brigade: Another attempt, this time by the 2/6th Warwicks, to take the enemy positions on Hill 35 was unsuccessful.

Tuesday 4 September

Temperature 71°F; clear. Rainfall: nil.

61st Division (XIX Corps)
182 Brigade: The 2/8th Warwicks attacked Aisne Farm and got to within 30 yards of it before being forced back.

58th Division (XIX Corps)
175 Brigade: A patrol occupied Spot Farm.

Wednesday 5 September

Temperature 74°F; clear. Rainfall: 5.1mm.

61st Division (XIX Corps)
'B' Company 2/6th Warwicks made an unsuccessful night attack on Hill 35; they captured an outpost but were later bombed out.

Thursday 6 September

Temperature 77°F; overcast. Rainfall: 24.6mm.

42nd Division (XV Corps)
125 Brigade, consisting of the 1/5th and 1/6th Lancashire Fusiliers, with the 1/7th and 1/8th in support, attacked the positions known as Iberian, Borry and Beck House Farms. Starting at 7.30 a.m., a company of the 1/6th managed to take Beck House but the two companies attacking Iberian Farm came under machine-gun fire from the southern slopes of Hill 35. At 10.45

RGA gunners serving a 13-pdr (9cwt) anti-aircraft gun on a Mark IV Motor Lorry Mounting (Thornycroft lorry) in September 1917. A shell is being placed in the breech. Note the telescope and rangefinder in foreground. (Q.11667)

a.m. the Germans launched a bombing counter-attack which re-took Beck House, killing or capturing all but two of the Fusiliers. This in turn exposed the other companies to fire from Hill 35 and forced them to withdraw to their original positions.

The 1/5th now had their flank exposed, and a German counter-attack at 7.30 p.m. forced them to fall back. The right flank, however, managed to hold on to 150 yards in advance of their original position, and consolidated.

61st Division (XIX Corps)
The 2/5th Warwicks made an unsuccessful night attack on Hill 35.

51st Division (XVIII Corps)
'A' Company of the 5th Seaforth Highlanders made an unsuccessful raid on Pheasant Trench.

Friday 7 September
Temperature 72°F; overcast. Rainfall: 0.1mm.

42nd Division (XV Corps)
125 Brigade relinquished the ground the 1/5th Lancashire Fusiliers had gained the previous day.

Saturday 8 September [26]
Temperature 72°F; fog. Rainfall: nil.

58th Division (XVIII Corps)
174 Brigade used the 2/6th and 2/8th Londons to raid a pillbox and fortified shell holes.

25th Division (II Corps)
The Division was relieved by the 47th Division (X Corps).

Sunday 9 September
Temperature 71°F; fog. Rainfall: nil.

24th Division (II Corps)
The Germans attacked Inverness Copse, but the position was retained after heavy fighting.

Monday 10 September
Temperature 66°F; clear. Rainfall: nil.

38th Division (XIV Corps)
Relieved by the 20th Division (XIV Corps).

[26]VC: Sgt John Carmichael.

Tuesday 11 September
Temperature 71°F; clear . Rainfall: nil.

42nd Division (XV Corps)
126 Brigade: During the night the 9th Manchesters launched an unsuccessful attack on a blockhouse called The Hut.[27]

Wednesday 12 September
Temperature 62°F; overcast. Rainfall: nil.

Nothing of significance happened on this day.

Thursday 13 September
Temperature 61°F; overcast. Rainfall: 1.7mm.

Guards Division[28] (XIV Corps)
The Germans[29] attacked posts on the north side of Broembeek and also the Wijdendrift road. The Guards were driven out and back to shell holes in the rear.

Friday 14 September
Temperature 66°F; overcast. Rainfall: 0.4mm.

58th Division (XVIII Corps)
At 3.00 a.m. the 2/1st Londons attacked Winnipeg from the direction of Springfield. At 7.30 p.m. 200 Germans counter-attacked Springfield.

Left, top: The ruins of the village of Poelcappelle on 13 September, showing two German concrete blockhouses destroyed by British gunfire, the large one in the distance still occupied by the enemy. (Q.3028)

Left, centre: German dead outside a captured pillbox. (Q.11663)

Left, bottom: Another view of the ruins of Poelcappelle. (Q.45462)

42nd Division (XV Corps)

126 Brigade advanced with the 1/4th East Lancs and dug a new trench 100 yards ahead of their old position.

Saturday 15 September

Temperature 67°F; overcast. Rainfall: 0.1mm.

47th Division (X Corps)

The 7th Londons attacked a strong-point[30] near Inverness Copse.

42nd Division (XV Corps)

126 Brigade attacked with the 1/4th East Lancs and took a point called Sans Souci.[31]

51st Division (XVIII Corps)

The Division launched a Chinese attack[32] utilizing dummy figures.

Sunday 16 September

Temperature 73°F; overcast. Rainfall: nil.

20th Division (XIV Corps)

A German counter-attack on the right flank was repulsed by small-arms fire.

Guards Division (XIV Corps)

The Germans launched an attack through Ney Copse, cutting off sixteen men of the 2nd Irish Guards, who managed to fight their way back to the British line.

47th Division (X Corps)

The Division resisted a counter-attack on Cryer Farm.

Monday 17 September

Temperature 67°F; overcast. Rainfall: nil.

47th Division (X Corps)

Relieved by the 1st and 2nd Australian Divisions (I ANZAC Corps).

Tuesday 18 September

Temperature 65°F; clear. Rainfall: 0.4mm.

Nothing of significance happened on this day.

Wednesday 19 September

Temperature 72°F; clear. Rainfall: 5.1mm.

Nothing of significance occurred on this day.

Thursday 20 September

Temperature 66°F; overcast. Rainfall: nil.

BATTLE OF THE MENIN ROAD RIDGE (20–25 September)

SECOND ARMY
IX Corps
19th Division

The Division attacked at 5.40 a.m. with two brigades.

58 Brigade attacked with the 6th Wiltshires, the 9th Welsh Regiment and the 9th Cheshires[33]; the 9th Royal Welsh Fusiliers were in support.

Considerable fire was encountered from south-west of Hessian Wood, Jarrocks Farm, Pioneer House, Hollebeke Château and the railway embankment. The Welsh were held up by fire from the wood and did not reach the first objective; the Wiltshires, therefore, formed a defensive flank on their left.

At 6.24 a.m. the advance continued. The Wiltshires had taken their final objective and formed a defensive flank on the left. The Welsh were held up in passing through Hessian Wood but went on to take the northern edge of it and gained touch with the Wilts at the south-western corner. Moat Farm and Funny Farm were also taken by the moppers-up.

57 Brigade attacked with the 10th Worcesters, the 8th Gloucesters and the 8th North Staffs; the 10th Royal Warwicks were in reserve. The Red Line was taken, although the muddy conditions slowed the Gloucesters and North Staffs and they came under fire from a row of dug-outs north of Top House. Considerable opposition was met from Wood Farm and Belgian Wood. The latter was cleared by a bayonet charge by the Gloucesters. The Blue Line was taken.

A liaison detachment consisting of half a platoon of the 8th North Staffs, a machine-gun detachment and the 16th Sherwood Foresters (117 Brigade, 39th Division) was ordered to establish posts near North Farm. This they managed to do after a short, sharp fight. Consolidation was hampered by fire from Hollebeke Château. A counter-attack on North Farm at 7.30 p.m. was destroyed by artillery, machine-gun and rifle fire.

X Corps
39th Division

The Division attacked at 5.40 a.m. with one brigade.

117 Brigade assaulted with the 17th Sherwood Foresters, supported by the 16th Sherwood Foresters[34] and the 16th Rifle Brigade[35]; the 17th King's Royal Rifle Corps were in reserve. On the right, the Foresters pushed on to the western edge of Bulgar Wood, taking a number of blockhouses on the way to

---

[27]A covering party found a wounded private of the Inniskilling Fusiliers who had been lying in no man's land since 11 August.
[28]VCs: L/Sgt John Moyney and Pte Thomas Woodcock.
[29]Two hundred Württembergers, most wearing armour.
[30]Later named Cryer Farm, after the officer who captured it.
[31]Not to be confused with Sans Souci Farm.
[32]A Chinese attack was a dummy attack using cut-out wooden figures—which could be raised or lowered—to deceive the enemy as to the direction of the attack.
[33]VC: 2/Lt Hugh Colvin.
[34]VC: Cpl Ernest Albert Egerton.
[35]VC: Sgt William Francis Burman.

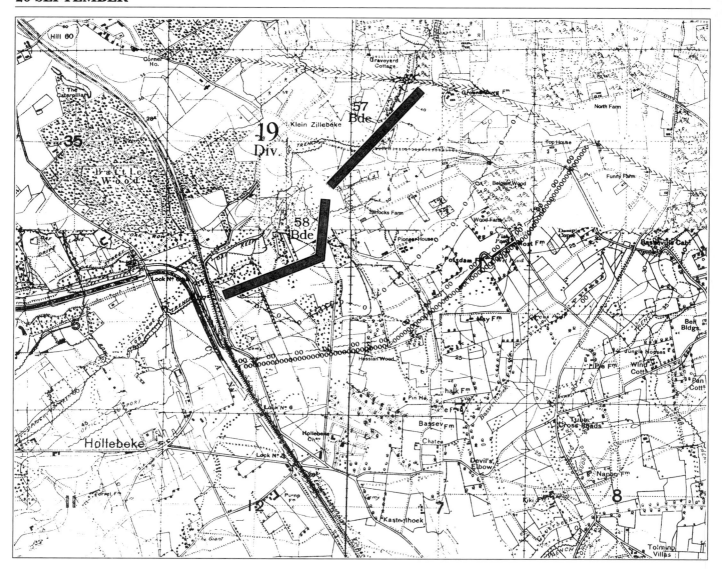

the Red Line. The Rifle Brigade came under fire almost immediately from blockhouses in the 41st Divisional area; they took two of them and pushed on to take the Red Line.

At 7 a.m. the advance continued. The KRRC cleared dug-outs on the way to taking the Blue Line while the Foresters came under fire from the north-east. By 7.45 a.m. the objective was reached and held. A defensive flank was pushed out by the KRRC to gain touch with the 41st Division. Touch was already gained with the 19th Division. At 6.30 p.m. the 1/6th Cheshires (118 Brigade) established a post beyond the Bassevillebeek.

German counter-attacks were made at 5.30, 7 and 9 p.m. but all were broken up by artillery and small-arms fire.

41st Division
The Division attacked at 5.40 a.m. with two brigades, plus one in close support.

122 Brigade attacked with the 18th KRRC supported by the 12th East Surreys and with the 15th Hampshire Regiment supported by the 11th Royal West Kents. The Hampshires at first made rapid progress until they came to Java Avenue, just in front of the first objective. This was eventually cleared by a rush and the first objective was taken by 6.15 a.m.

The Rifles were held up for an hour by fire from a pillbox 150 yards east of Bodmin Copse. The pillbox was dealt with by rifle grenades and the ridge was then taken. The Rifles moved on to their objective just short of the Bassevillebeek by 6.15 a.m. The attack continued with 'B' and 'D' Companies Royal West Kents giving support; the second objective fell with little resistance and the Hampshires consolidated. The West Kents went forward, past Tower Hamlets (which was a mass of concrete dug-outs and pillboxes) and on to take Tower Trench. They could not hold it, however, and were forced to fall back to 150 yards in front of the second objective and linked up with the East Surreys.

At 6.40 p.m. the 15th Hampshire Regiment[36] succeeded in capturing

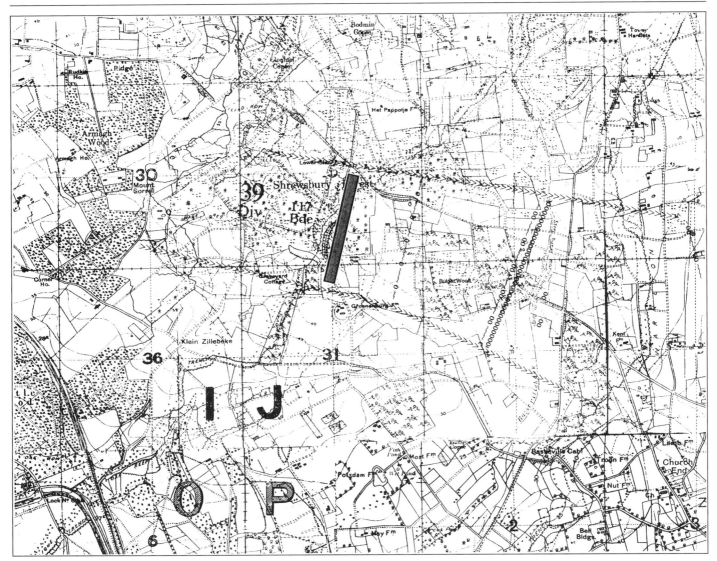

The Battle of the Menin Road Ridge: digging out wounded from the 13th Durham Light Infantry Regimental Aid Post near Zillebeke which had been blown in by a shell, 20 September. (Q.5980)

their objective, the Green Line, and gained touch with 68 Brigade (23rd Division).

124 Brigade attacked with the 10th Queen's and the 21st KRRC; the 32nd Royal Fusiliers and the 26th Royal Fusiliers were both in support. The Queen's came under fire almost immediately from two machine guns. These were outflanked and captured and the Queen's went on to take both

[36]VC: 2/Lt Montague Shadworth Seymour Moore.

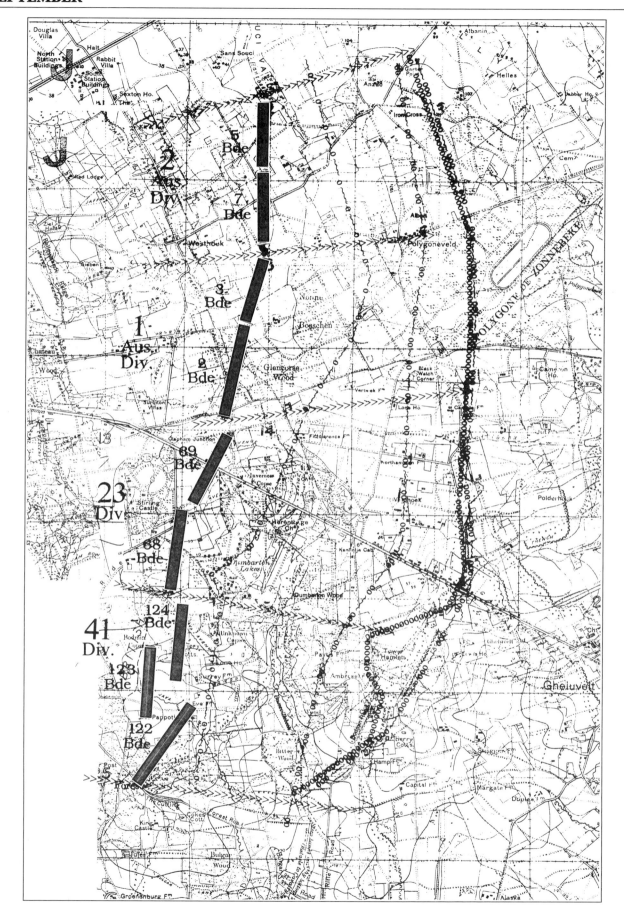

of their objectives, the Red and Blue Lines, thus allowing 123 Brigade to pass through and attack the Green Line.

123 Brigade: At 8.30 a.m. the Brigade went through 124 Brigade and crossed Bassevillebeek. They stormed the slope of Tower Hamlets and were finally brought to a halt on the plateau by machine-gun fire from Bodmin Road. They dug in just short of the objective.

At 4.30 p.m. another attack was launched with the 23rd Middlesex, 10th Royal West Kents and 20th Durham Light Infantry. The Middlesex were held up for a time by machine guns and snipers on a ridge to their front; this was cleared by artillery. By 6.30 p.m. they had reached the ridge and blockhouses. They pushed on to the Bassevillebeek and secured their objective, the Blue Line. By this time the Middlesex were too weak in numbers to push on to the third objective and consolidated where they were. At 8 p.m. the Germans were seen massing for a counter-attack but were dispersed by small-arms fire.

23rd Division

The Division attacked at 5.40 a.m. with two brigades.

68 Brigade attacked with the 10th and 11th Northumberland Fusiliers and the 13th Durham Light Infantry; the 12th Durham Light Infantry were in support. The 11th Northumberlands came under fire from a strongpoint in Dumbarton Wood, which they took after a sharp fight. A platoon of Northumberlands advanced with the 11th West Yorkshires (69 Brigade), who went on and captured Herenthage Château. The rest of the Battalion reached the Red Line more or less on time.

The 10th Northumberland Fusiliers took over the attack on the second objective and succeeded in taking the Blue Line, its left holding Kantinje Cabaret. The 12th Durhams, although in support, became involved in the fighting.

The 13th Durham Light Infantry attacked at 9.53 a.m. across the Menin Road at Tower Hamlets and were engaged by the Germans in the buildings along the road which anchored their flank. They pushed on and took their final objective.

69 Brigade attacked with the 11th West Yorkshire Regiment, 9th Yorkshire Regiment and 10th Duke of Wellington's. The 11th attacked Inverness Copse and, with the help of 69th Trench

The Battle of the Menin Road Ridge: a dressing station at Potijze Château, 20 September, showing some of the hundreds of wounded German prisoners who passed through it during the morning of the combined attack by British, Australian and South African troops. (Q.2848)

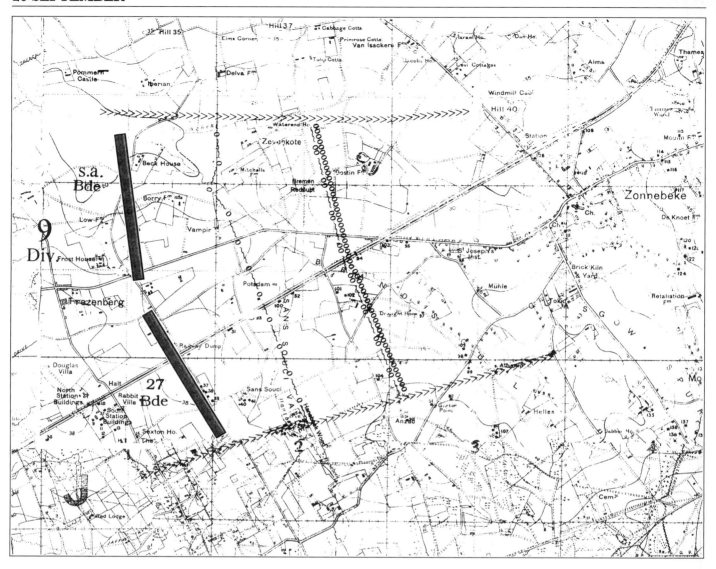

Mortar Battery, managed to take the objective. By 6.10 a.m. they had started to consolidate.

The 9th Yorks met difficulty in moving up through the Copse: they lost direction because of the smoke and dust and took casualties from Germans missed in the mopping up. 'A' and 'B' Companies' task was to clear a line of pillboxes and dugouts extending southwards from a concrete tower situated about the centre of the German line to a small pond just north of the Menin Road, and this was accomplished. 'C' and 'D' Companies passed through and went on to take the Blue Line. Consolidation was begun.

'B' and 'D' Companies of the 10th Duke of Wellington's and a company of the 8th Yorkshire Regiment took Northampton Farm with ease. Behind it, however, was a string of twelve pillboxes. These caused many casualties but they were nevertheless taken and cleared. 'A' and 'C' Companies of the 10th Duke of Wellington's met resistance from the concrete dug-outs of Veldhoek and from a strongly held hedge which covered them; these, however, fell. The Green Line was taken and the left flank was in touch with the Australians.

The Division faced two counterattacks, one at 2.45 p.m. from south of the Reutelbeek and the other at 3 p.m. from the railway cutting north of Gheluvelt. Both were dispersed by artillery fire.

I ANZAC Corps
1st Australian Division

The Division attacked at 5.40 a.m.
2 Australian Brigade: The 6th Battalion[37] attacked with the 5th Battalion in support. The 8th and 7th Battalions were to pass through and take the third objective.

The 6th crossed Glencorse Wood with little difficulty. Machine guns opened up from the southern edge of the wood but were soon dealt with. Subjected to rifle grenades, the German garrison at Fitzclarence Farm were forced to keep their heads down and the position was taken from the rear.

The attack was taken over by the 5th Battalion; the pillboxes on their front mostly surrendered without a shot be-

The 9th and 10th Brigades assaulted the Green Line, which fell easily and was consolidated.

2nd Australian Division

The Division attacked at 5.40 a.m. *7 Australian Brigade* attacked with the 25th Battalion; the 27th Battalion were in support and the 28th in reserve. The 25th advanced through the swampy Hanebeek, met little opposition and moved on to the first objective, the Red Line. The 27th took over the attack on the Blue Line: attacking the pillbox Albert, and capturing it easily, they went on to consolidate their objective. *5 Australian Brigade* attacked with the 20th Battalion and the 18th Battalion in support; the 17th and 26th Battalions were in reserve. The attack went well, although the left of the 20th met some resistance from a line of old concrete artillery shelters, causing a slight hold-up. They went on to the first objective but, whilst attempting to consolidate, came under fire from two pillboxes 200 yards away. To save further casualties, these were dealt with on the spot.

The 18th Battalion took over the attack on the Blue Line, taking Iron Cross and Anzac House in its stride. The 18th were then forced to take Garter Point to prevent sniping on troops consolidating the Blue Line.

The third objective, the Green Line, was assaulted by the 17th and 28th Battalions (7 Brigade), with the 26th Battalion in support, and was taken easily.

FIFTH ARMY
V Corps
9th Division

The Division attacked at 5.40 a.m. with the 27th and the South African Brigades.

Australian troops rescuing an officer whose parachute has become entangled with the branches of a tree on his descent from a balloon near Zillebeke on 20 September. One man is climbing the trunk of the tree. (Q.5983)

ing fired. They did, however, outflank a blockhouse which was causing the 23rd Division some difficulty and then went on to the Blue Line, taking Verbeek Farm on the way. Consolidation began, but they were fired on from Black Watch Corner. A party was sent out to take the pillbox, and it managed this with little difficulty.

The 7th and 8th Battalions took the Green Line, encountering little resistance, and went on to consolidate the position.

3 Australian Brigade: The 11th Battalion attacked with the 12th Battalion in support; the 10th[38] and 9th Battalions were to take the third objective. They met problems from concrete shelters along the sunken track at the northern side of Glencorse Wood. The Germans erected a machine gun on the roof of one of the shelters which momentarily held up the attack but was soon dealt with by the 11th and 10th Battalions. The assault battalions carried on to the second objective across Nonne Bosschen by using the edges of shell craters. The Red Line was just east of Glencorse Wood. The second objective—the western edge of Polygon Wood—was gained by the 12th Battalion by 7.45 a.m.

---

[37]VC: 2/Lt Frederick Birks.
[38]VC: Pte Reginald Roy Inwood.

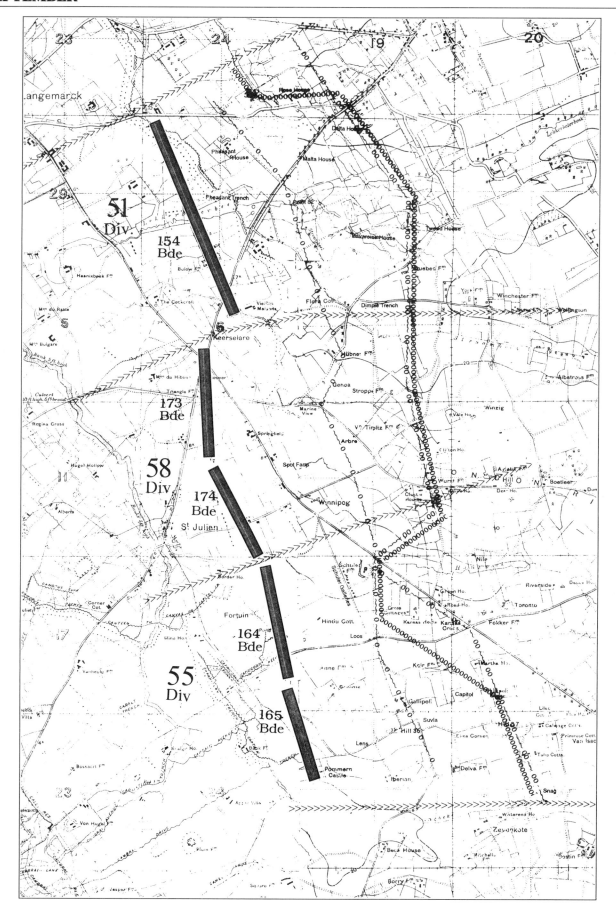

Left, upper: A British padre and a doctor attend to wounded German prisoners after the attack on Potsdam (a German stronghold near Zonnebeke). Potijze, 20 September 1917. (Q.2856)

Left, lower: A trench with pillboxes captured by the 9th Division in the Battle of the Menin Road Ridge, 20 September. (Q.11684)

Lines was carried on by the 1st and 2nd Battalions. The 1st Battalion reached their objective without any opposition but the 2nd came under fire from positions in the 55th Division area, namely Waterend House, Tulip Cottages and Hill 37. The 2nd took Zevenkote and Bremen Redoubt with difficulty. They then threw out a defensive flank to the south bank of the Zonnebeke stream, until the 55th Division caught up with them.

The Division then consolidated its objectives. An enemy counter-attack at 5 p.m. was stopped by artillery.

55th Division

165 Brigade attacked with the 1/7th and 1/9th King's Liverpool Regiment; the 1/5th and 1/6th King's were to take the Green Line. The 1/7th King's soon came under fire from Iberian and Hill 35. Iberian fell at 6.45 a.m., and by 7 a.m. the Red Line had been taken and consolidation had begun. The companies reorganized and set off to the second objective, taking Delva Farm convincingly and reaching the Green Line by 8.30 a.m.

At 9.45 a.m. two companies of the 1/5th North Lancs were ordered to reinforce the 1/6th and 1/9th King's in an attack on Hill 37 from Hill 35. At 3.35 p.m. British troops were seen advancing on the Hill and at 5.10 p.m. the position was being consolidated. The right of the 1/9th King's immediately came under fire from Lens but this was soon dealt with. On the left,

27 Brigade attacked with the 6th King's Own Scottish Borderers and the 9th Scottish Rifles; the 12th Royal Scots[39] were in support. Attacking at zero hour, the KOSB rushed Hanebeek Wood and continued on to the Green Line. The right was held up by a strong position on the Railway consisting of several pillboxes and was covered by the Potsdam group of pillboxes on the left. A company of the 12th Royal Scots was detailed to deal with them

all, and did so successfully. The Red Line was taken on time. The second objective, the Green Line including the Zonnebeke Redoubt, fell easily.
South African Brigade: The leading battalions were the 3rd and 4th Regiments supported by the 1st and 2nd[40]. The Red Line was taken in their stride, with the 3rd Regiment assisting the Royal Scots in taking Potsdam, while the 4th Battalion entered Borry Farm. The assault on the Blue and Green

[39]VC: T/Capt Henry Reynolds.
[40]VC: L-Cpl William Henry Hewitt.

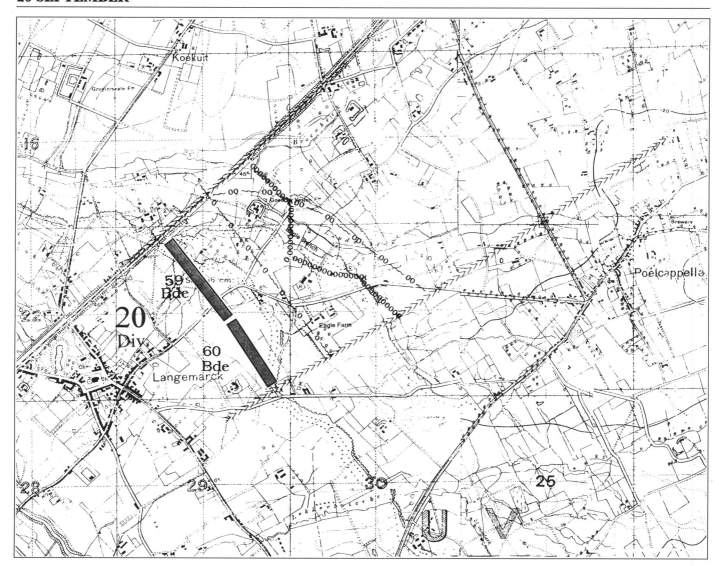

opposition came from Gallipoli which was taken by 8 a.m. along with Keir Farm dug-outs and the Capitol. Several strongpoints in the vicinity of Hill 35 were still holding out. The 1/9th King's were ordered to clear this area and Suvla, and they managed this successfully. Between 2 and 2.30 p.m. a counter-attack was repulsed by British artillery fire.

164 Brigade: The 1/4th King's Own (R Lancs) became intermixed with the 1/4th Loyal North Lancs in the neighbourhood of Aisne Farm owing to the

A Royal Scots stretcher-bearer attending to a wounded soldier and taking down particulars for the next-of-kin. Near Potijze, 20 September. (Q.2851)

A German prisoner captured in the attack on Vampire Farm by Scottish and South African troops. Near Potijze, 20 September. (Q.2860)

condition of the ground and the troops failed to sort themselves out. Part of the Loyals became involved in the capture of Gallipoli, but only isolated parties reached the leading lines of the 1/4th King's Own occupying the Red Line. The 1/5th King's Own (R Lancs) became intermingled with other units and were therefore concentrated in the vicinity of Loos, to guard against counter-attacks.

The 2/5th Lancashire Fusiliers, in the centre, came under heavy fire from the front and the left flank and lost 50 per cent of their men before reaching Schuler Galleries. On taking their part of the Galleries they moved on and elements reached the Green Line.

On the left, the 1/8th King's had a similar experience. The Battalion was engaged at the northern end of Schuler Galleries, which did not fall until the southern end fell to the 2/5th Lancs[41].

At 8.15 p.m. the situation was as follows: 164 Brigade held the Dotted Red Line, with posts in shell holes etc as far forward as the Green Line; and 165 Brigade held the Snag and Hill 37.

XVIII Corps
58th Division
The Division attacked with two brigades at 5.40 a.m.

174 Brigade attacked with the 2/8th London[42], 2/5th London and 2/6th London in series. The 2/8th, attacking the first objective, cleared the strongpoints in front of Vancouver Farm and Keerselare, the only resistance coming from Hübner Farm. The 2/5th and 2/6th went on to outflank Hübner Farm and take Dimple Trench. The 2/6th took up the Divisional attack and took Cluster House and Clifton House. Olive House was occupied, as was Wurst Farm, the final objective. The line of Marine View, Genoa, Hübner

and Flora Cottage was consolidated in touch with the 2/4th London (173 Brigade) and the 9th Royal Scots (51st Division) on the flanks.

173 Brigade's task was to advance 1,000 yards and take the strongpoints on the western edge of the Gravenstafel spur. The 2/4th London achieved this and went on to occupy Winnipeg crossroads.

51st Division
The Division attacked with one brigade.

154 Brigade advanced with the 9th Royal Scots on the Blue Dotted Line and the 4th Seaforth Highlanders taking the Blue Line with the 7th Argyll & Sutherland Highlanders and the 4th Gordon Highlanders. Attacking at 5.40 a.m. the Royal Scots, whilst meeting strong resistance in and around Pheasant Trench, moved on to take Flora Cottage. They came under fire from Hübner Farm in the 58th Division area. Lewis guns were sent to help the Londoners capture the Farm. The Scots went on and took their objective, the

Blue Line. The Seaforths were also held up at Pheasant Trench but cleared it and consolidated the Blue Line. The 7th A&SH also took the Blue Line, and, on the way, Flora Cottage, Quebec Farm and Bavaroise House. The 4th Gordons' advance continued, encountering resistance from Pheasant Farm Cemetery and also Malta, Rose and Delta Houses. However, they reached the Blue Line.

At 5 p.m. a counter-attack between York Farm and Tweed House was fought off until a shortage of ammunition forced a retirement. Rose House continued to hold out after the the front line was broken. The 8th Argyll & Sutherland Highlanders, on the north of the Lekkerboterbeek, held out against numerous counter-attacks.

On the right, the 7th Argyll & Sutherland Highlanders and two platoons of the 8th and 4th Seaforths formed defensive flanks, creating a 'V' shape which caught the enemy in crossfire.

[41]Schuler Farm did not itself fall until 4.30 p.m. the next day, when it was taken by the 1/8th.
[42]VC: Sgt Alfred Joseph Knight.

Right, top: A much-battered male
Mark IV tank on the Ypres battlefield,
September 1917. (Q.11685)

Right, centre: A knocked-out female
Mark IV tank, armed with machine
guns, on the Ypres battlefield,
September 1917. (Q.11682)

Right, bottom: A tank in difficult
conditions near Westhoek, 21 September. (E[AUS].1421)

The troops which had withdrawn were
rallied after collecting ammunition
from the dead and wounded. They
counter-attacked and won back the
lost ground and, at its furthest, Point 82
on the Poelcappelle road.

XIV Corps
20th Division

At zero hour oil drums were fired at
Eagle Trench[43]. They fell beyond the
trench, doing little more than light up
the assaulting troops.

60 Brigade attacked at 5.40 a.m. with
the 12th Rifle Brigade and the 6th Ox
& Bucks; the 6th King's Shropshire
Light Infantry were in support. The
left of the Brigade was held up by Eagle
Farm. The advance succeeded in taking all but the northern part of Eagle
Trench immediately east of Schreiboom crossroads. The barrage was re-
scheduled and, at 6.30 p.m., the attack
was re-launched. It was very much a
repeat of the morning's events except
that smoke was fired at Eagle Trench,
which this time fell and was occupied.

59 Brigade attacked at 5.40 a.m. with
the 11th and 10th King's Royal Rifle
Corps; the 11th Rifle Brigade were in
support and the 10th Rifle Brigade in
reserve. On the left the Brigade carried
the trench line and advanced as far as
the 't Goed ter Vesten Farm. In the
second attack the 11th Rifle Brigade
replaced the 11th KRRC. To the front
of the 11th Rifle Brigade the smoke
was not effective and they suffered
accordingly from machine-gun fire.
Losing 66 per cent of the troops engaged, they were not able to take Eagle

Trench in its entirety: a small portion remained in enemy hands, forming a pronounced salient, although the rest of the trench was occupied by the Division. At 8.30 a.m. a counter-attack on Eagle Trench was driven off by small-arms fire.

Above: A German strongpoint at Nonne Bosschen, 21 September. The wheels are from a light Minenwerfer. (E[AUS].867)

Below: Marshland between Hanebeek and Nonne Bosschen over which Australian troops passed in the advance to their second objective, 21 September. (E[AUS].909)

Friday 21 September

Temperature 62°F; 25% cloud cover. Rainfall: nil.

Guards Division (XIV Corps)
Relieved by the 29th Division (XIV Corps).

41st Division (X Corps)
123 Brigade attacked with the 10th Royal West Kents and the 20th Durham Light Infantry. The 23rd Middlesex were in reserve. Little headway was made owing to the boggy conditions, and the advance consisted of a series of short rushes until the Copse on the Bassevillebeek was reached, a forward line of posts was put out and the position was consolidated.

During the afternoon a number of counter-attacks were launched by the Germans but all were repulsed. At 7 p.m. five waves of Germans were seen advancing towards the Brigade but were dispersed by artillery and small-arms fire.

Saturday 22 September

Temperature 63°F; clear. Rainfall: nil.

9th Division (V Corps)
Relieved by the 3rd Division (V Corps).

Sunday 23 September

Temperature 65°F; 25% cloud cover. Rainfall: nil.

8th Division (II Corps)
The enemy unsuccessfully raided Van and Zero posts.

---

[43]A trench which ran between two solid embankments about 8 feet high.

Left: A derelict Mark IV tank. The men in the foreground are in a gunpit trench and a Vickers machine-gun tripod can be seen in the centre of the photograph. East of Zillebeke, 22 September. (Q.11678)

Right, top: A German concrete emplacement smashed by British gun-fire near Zonnebeke, 23 September. (Q.2891)

Right, centre: German dead outside a concrete emplacement near Zonne-beke, 23 September. (Q.2893)

Right, bottom: German dead at the entrance of a dug-out destroyed by gunfire near Zonnebeke, 23 September. Note the grenades in the storage hole, behind the shovel. (Q.3116)

41st Division (X Corps)

Relieved by 39th Division (X Corps).

23rd Division (X Corps)

Relief by the 33rd Division (X Corps) was begun.

98 Brigade (33rd Division) co-operated with the 1st Australian Division (I ANZAC Corps) in re-taking the front line.

58th Division (XVIII Corps)

An enemy attack was launched against Stroppe Farm but failed.

51st Division (XVIII Corps)

At 7 p.m., following an afternoon bombardment, a heavy German counter-attack was launched from the direction of Poelcappelle against the centre of the Division. It was broken up by artillery and small-arms fire from the 6th and 5th Seaforths.

20th Division (XIV Corps)

The Division was attacked by the Germans at 6.25 a.m. but the latter were driven off by small-arms fire.

59 Brigade: At 7 a.m. the 12th King's Royal Rifle Corps and the 10th Rifle Brigade attacked Eagle Trench under cover of trench mortar fire. By sending parties of bombers from both ends and a covering party in front of the trench, the Brigade cleared the salient after a sharp fight.

Monday 24 September

Temperature 74°F; 50% cloud cover. Rainfall: nil.

Nothing of significance happened on this day.

Tuesday 25 September

Temperature 75°F; mist. Rainfall: nil.

23rd Division (X Corps)

The relief of the 23rd Division by the 33rd Division (X Corps) continued. During the relief the Germans counter-attacked along the whole Divisional front.

100 Brigade (33rd Division): At 5.30 a.m. the 1st Queen's and part of the 9th Highland Light Infantry were driven back and the Germans occupied the position. On the left the 2nd Worcesters and the 4th King's (98 Brigade, 33rd Division) lost no ground.

At 9 a.m. a company of the Queen's was able to push forward and retake the original support line and at the same time the HLI succeeded in recap-turing part of the ground lost on their right. Meanwhile small-arms fire from the Worcesters and King's brought any attempt by the enemy to improve his position to a halt.

51st Division (XVIII Corps)

Relieved by the 11th Division (XVIII Corps).

Wednesday 26 September

Temperature 68°F; mist. Rainfall: 0.5mm.

BATTLE OF POLYGON WOOD (26 September–3 October)

X Corps
39th Division

The Division attacked at 5.50 a.m. with two brigades.

118 Brigade attacked with the 1/1st Cambridgeshires and the 4/5th Black Watch; the 1/6th Cheshire Regiment was in support. The assaulting battalions met extremely boggy ground and only 'A' Company of the Cambridge-shires was able to keep up with the barrage. By the time 'C' and 'D' Companies had cleared the western edge of Joist Redoubt, 'A' Company was en-

gaged on the eastern edge. A gap developed between the Cambridgeshires and the Sussex on the left, but this was subsequently filled. All the objectives were taken, apart from a large pillbox on the left of the front.

116 Brigade attacked with the 14th Hampshire Regiment and the 13th Royal Sussex; the 11th and 12th Royal Sussex were in support. The Brigade advanced through Tower Hamlets, took all their objectives and joined the Cambridgeshire Regiment (118 Brigade) who were consolidating the objectives on a line just behind Tower Trench with a post in the north-western corner of Gheluvelt Wood.

33rd Division

The task of the Division was to attack with only 98 Brigade covering the flank of the Australians and 100 Brigade regaining the ground lost on the previous day.

100 Brigade attacked with the 1/9th Highland Light Infantry[44] and the 1st Queen's in the lead. The Queen's were halted 50 yards short of their objective and one company of the 1st Cameronians (19 Brigade) was sent to help. By 9 a.m. the Queen's reported that they had made contact with the Sussex (116 Brigade, 39th Division) on their right. At 2.30 p.m. the Germans attempted to counter-attack the Queen's left flank, but two platoons of the HLI charged, drove them off and carried on across open ground to regain another portion of their lost ground. With the exception of one pillbox near the Menin Road, the whole of the ground lost on the 25th had been recaptured. At 4 p.m. the pillbox, too, fell, to a party of Cameronians.

At 5 p.m. the Germans launched a counter-attack, but this was stopped by artillery fire. A large party of Germans was observed running for shelter towards a pillbox which was clearly too

[44] VC: A/L-Cpl John Brown Hamilton.

Top left: Two artillery officers during a quiet spell at Zillebeke, 24 September. (Q.6016)

Top centre: Men of the Highland Light Infantry rest by the roadside on the way up to attack during the Battle of the Menin Road Ridge, 24 September. (Q.6006)

Above left: Preparing to explode a dud German shell near Zillebeke with two blocks of pressed guncotton charge, 24 September. (Q.6017)

Above right: The Battle of Polygon Wood: men travel by light railway to the front line. Pilckem Ridge, 25 September. (Q.5998)

small to hold them, and many were shot down as they struggled to get inside.

On the left, the 4th King's were on their original line by 1.30 p.m. They pushed out posts across the Reutelbeek and tried to gain touch with the Scot-

500 yards and take forward with them the troops still holding Black Watch Corner from the previous day's fighting.

Earlier, at 2.20 a.m., the Scottish Rifles had reached a line north and south through Jerk House and were in touch with the Australians on their left. The Suffolks were caught in a German barrage and the attack was put back until 5.30 a.m., but this time the shelling had become intense. The British barrage was lost and they were only able to join up with the troops at Black Watch Corner, some 1,000 yards short of the objective.

The 2nd Royal Welsh Fusiliers (19 Brigade) were sent up to help 98 Brigade. They moved into the Australian Divisional area in Polygon Wood and then attacked south-east at noon in co-operation with an attack from the Black Watch Corner line. Most of the ground lost on the previous day was regained.

I ANZAC Corps
5th Australian Division

The Division attacked with two brigades.

Above: A Foden steam wagon near Zillebeke, 24 September. (Q.6014)

15 Australian Brigade: The 59th Battalion was to take the first objective but the 29th and 31st[45] Battalions pushed on and got mixed up with them. The Brigade paused when the Germans showed some resistance at two pillboxes on the south-west corner of Polygon Wood, and came to a halt on the so-called racecourse[46], 150 yards short of the first objective.

The 31st Battalion came under fire from blockhouses on their right in the 33rd Divisional area. They extended their flank and came under fire from Cameron House. At 7.30 a.m. it was considered inadvisable to continue without the 33rd Division. Contact was thus made with the 33rd Division, and at 11 a.m. the 31st and 29th Battalions continued to the second objective. *14 Australian Brigade* attacked with the 53rd Battalion; the 56th and 55th Battalions were in support. The 53rd advanced without opposition and reached

tish Rifles (19 Brigade) but were unable to find any troops in the vicinity.
98 Brigade attacked with the 1/4th Suffolk and the 5/6th Scottish Rifles (attached from the 19th Brigade in Divisional Reserve). The Brigade were to start at 5.15 a.m. in order to cross the

[45]VC: Pte Patrick Joseph Budgen.
[46]A driving track of a former Belgian artillery school.

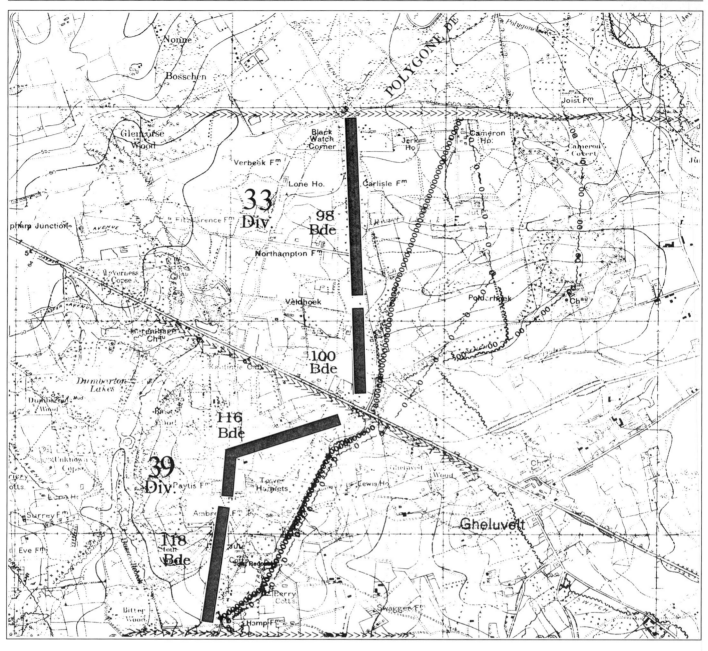

Top: An 18pdr shell dump on Pilckem Ridge, showing plank track for the use of limbers, 25 September. (Q.6010)

Above: Cavalry horses tethered behind a line of dug-outs in a dip in the ground near Clapham Junction (in

front of Zillebeke), 26 September. (Q.6018)

Left: Looking towards Glencorse Wood and Inverness Copse during the German counter-attack at Westhoek, 26 September. (E[AUS].916)

the Butte, which they bombed and captured. The attack was taken up by the 56th and 55th Battalions, who went well until encountering fire from the German headquarters on the Polygonebeek. The attack was held up until the 29th Battalion (15th Brigade) caught

up and cleared it. Pushing on, they came under fire from two pillboxes, which were eventually accounted for by the 56th Battalion.

Artillery and machine-gun fire dispersed the Germans before they could launch a counter-attack.

4th Australian Division

The Division attacked at 6.45 a.m. with the 4th and 13th Brigades, their objectives being the Red and Blue Lines.[47]

4 Australian Brigade[48] attacked in a mist with the 16th Battalion, while the 15th and 14th Battalions were in support. The 16th took their first objective, the Red Line, and were in touch with 14 Australian Brigade on their right. The

[47]The attacking troops had the colours of their objectives painted on the backs of their helmets.
[48]VC: Sgt John James Dwyer.

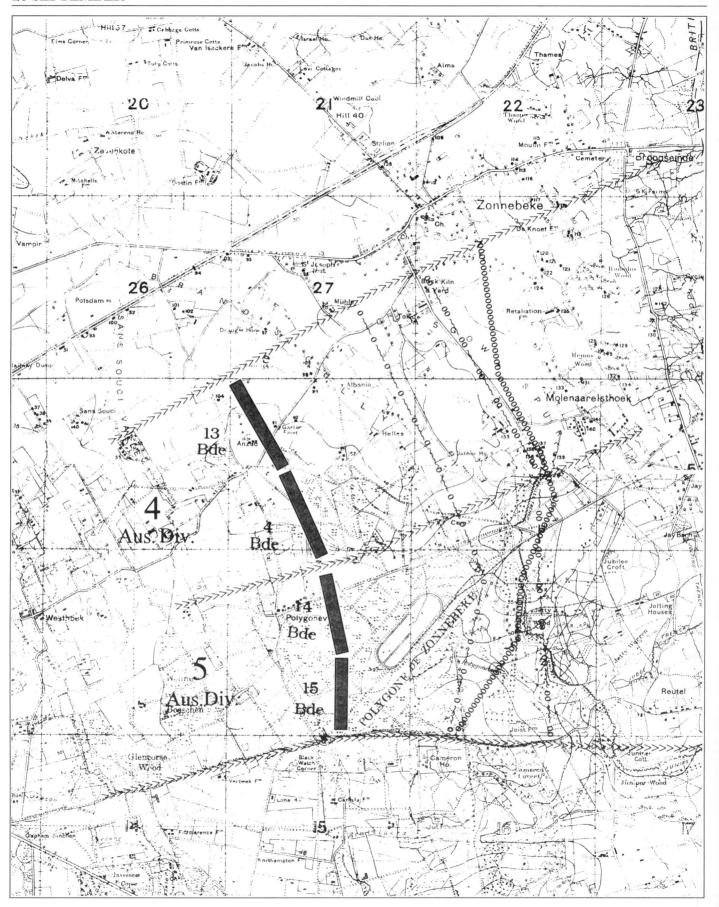

first counter-attack was spotted at 3 p.m. with the Germans massing on their front. This was dispersed by artillery fire.

13 Australian Brigade attacked with the 50th Battalion; the 49th and 51st Battalions were in support. The 50th captured two machine guns and nineteen prisoners on their way to the Red Line and moved on to the Blue Line. Advancing, and meeting little opposition, the 51st occupied the brickyard at Zonnebeke, in touch with the British 3rd Division on their left.

At 4 p.m., and again at 6 p.m., the Germans were reported massing on their front, but the threat was broken up by artillery fire.

V Corps
3rd Division
The Division attacked at 5.50 a.m., zero hour.

Above: RMA personnel load a 15-inch Mark II howitzer named *Grannie* near Ypres, September 1917. (Q.11661)

Below: Hauling a shell up to *Grannie*'s breech during the Battle of Polygon Wood. (Q.11664)

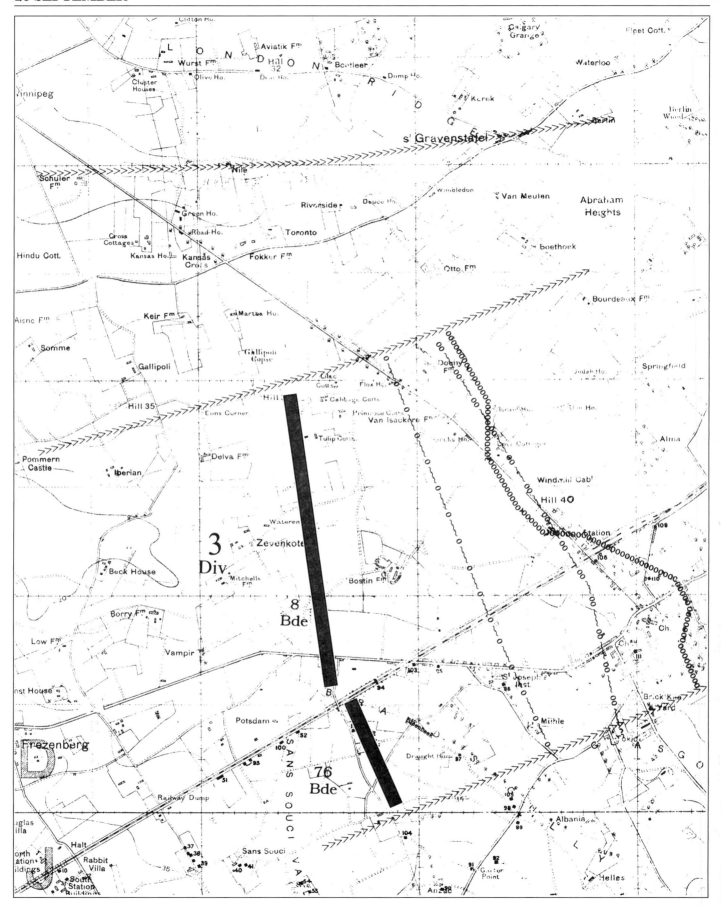

76th Brigade: On the right of the railway, the 2nd Suffolks and the 10th Royal Welsh Fusiliers advanced. Whilst encountering little resistance, they were briefly held up as they sought a crossing point over the Steenbeek, but they carried on to the Green Line. After the railway had been crossed the attack lost momentum under heavy machine-gun fire from the station. The centre of Zonnebeke was entered by parties of the RWF and the Suffolks but the station held out and they could only get to within 200 yards of it.

At 2.30 p.m. the first counter-attack was launched but this was easily repulsed. A more determined attack was made at 6.30 p.m. but was stopped with rifle and machine-gun fire.

The 2nd Suffolks held the Blue Line from the brickyard to Zonnebeke Church; the 10th RWF held 150 yards of the road running north-west from the church; the 8th King's Own held a line between Tokio and St Joseph's Institute; and 1st Gordons held a line between the Institute and the railway. *8 Brigade* attacked at 5.30 a.m. in a ground mist. The 2nd Royal Scots and the 8th East Yorks led with the 1st Royal Scots Fusiliers, and the 7th KSLI were in support. The Scots, with their right flank on the railway, took the first objective. The East Yorks came across some particularly marshy ground and were forced to split up to by-pass the flooded area. However, their objective, the Red Line, was reported taken by 7 a.m. The Scots and KSLI took over the advance and went on to take the western slopes of Hill 40, just short of the Blue Line. An unsuccessful attempt to take Hill 40 was made at 6.30 p.m.

The enemy counter-attacked but were repulsed. Another counter-attack forced back the leading troops, but a

The storming of Zonnebeke by the 3rd Division: a view of the battlefield, showing casualties of a Highland Regiment. (Q.11657)

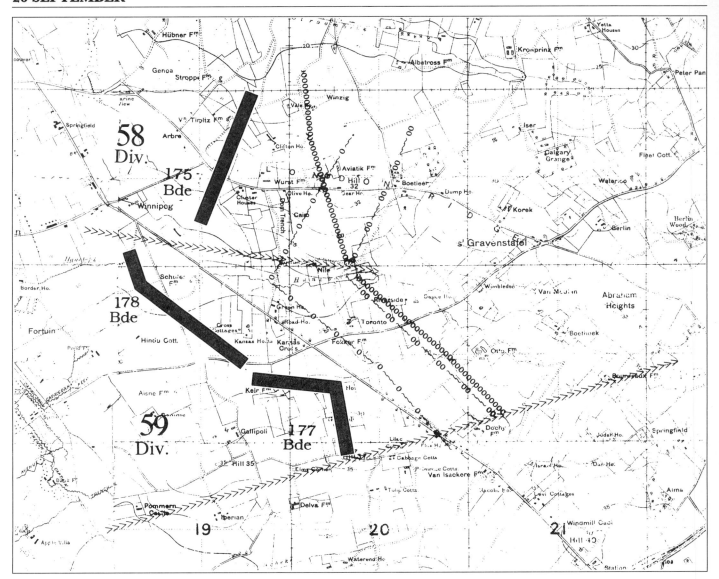

British counter-attack was made by the 12th West Yorks, who re-took nearly all the lost ground.

59th Division

The Division attacked with two brigades.

177 Brigade attacked with the 2/4th and 2/5th Leicesters, with the 2/4th and 2/5th Lincolns in support. Both battalions of Leicesters took their first objective, carried on until held up by their own barrage and dug in around Dochy Farm. 'B' Company of the 2/5th Lincolns took the farm, and the position was consolidated.

The Leicesters reported that they had taken their first objective by 7.50 a.m. Having met little serious opposition, they went on and took their final objective. It was decided by the Divisional commander to attempt to take Riverside and Otto Farms. Both objectives were captured, but, as the protective barrage was dropping short, Riverside Farm was abandoned.

178 Brigade attacked with the 2/6th and 2/7th Sherwood Foresters and, for the third objective, the 2/5th and 2/8th Sherwood Foresters with the 2/5th North Staffs (176 Brigade) in reserve. The attack went well, with the following blockhouses falling: Schuler Farm, Cross Cottages, Kansas House, Martha House, Green House, Road House, Kansas Cross and Focker. On the way to the second objective, Riverside, Toronto and Deuce House fell.

Between 5.30 and 6.50 p.m. both brigades reported an enemy attack. Some of the advance posts gave way in front of it, while the detachment at Otto Farm were in danger of being cut off when the right of the 177th Brigade fell back after repelling the attack. Reinforcements were brought up to strengthen the entire front and reoccupy Otto Farm. By 11 p.m. both brigades reported the situation restored and normal.

A conspicuous pillbox just south-east of Anzac Ridge, 28 September. (E[AUS].898)

XVIII Corps
58th Division

The Division attacked at 5.50 a.m. in a thick mist with one brigade.

175 Brigade attacked in support of the 59th Division, with the 2/9th London Regiment and 'B' Company of the 2/12th London Regiment. With their right along the Hanebeek valley, the attackers lost direction and came under fire from Dom Trench and a pill-box called Cairo. Both fell and the Division eventually came to a halt a quarter of a mile short of its objective, holding Dear House, Aviatik Farm and Vale House.

Later in the day a strong German counter-attack forced troops out of Aviatik Farm and Dear House. Elements of 175 Brigade counter-attacked but failed to recapture these positions.

The 2/12th London took their objective but were unable to make contact with the 2/9th and fell back to secure their flank. At 6.11 a.m. 'C' Company advanced and went on to take Nile, their objective. The line held was Vale House–Clifton House–just short of Aviatik Farm–Nile.

The enemy was seen in the direction of Korek, feeding troops down towards Riverside and Otto. The Germans were stopped by machine-gun and artillery barrages.

Thursday 27 September
Temperature 67°F; overcast. Rainfall: nil.

39th Division (X Corps)

Three German counter-attacks were broken up by artillery fire. That night the Division was relieved by 37th Division (IX Corps).

33rd Division (X Corps)

100 Brigade: At 5.40 a.m. it was reported that Cameron House had fallen, and the 2nd Royal Welsh Fusiliers (19 Brigade) were sent to fill the gap between the 4th King's and their right. This they did, and pushed on to the Blue Line.

98 Brigade attacked once more to plug the gap which existed between the Division and 15 Australian Brigade (5th Australian Division). Fierce and confused fighting continued until 3.50 p.m., when it was reported that they were in touch with the Australians at Cameron Covert.

That night the Division was relieved by the 23rd Division (X Corps).

3rd Division (V Corps)

Following an intense barrage, the Germans launched a counter-attack in the vicinity of Bostin Farm. The attack was repulsed but the troops of 9 Brigade were very badly shaken.

Friday 28 September
Temperature 65°F; 25% cloud cover. Rainfall: nil.

58th Division (XVIII Corps)

Relieved by the 48th Division (XVIII Corps).

20th Division (XIV Corps)

Relieved by the 29th Division (XIV Corps).

Saturday 29 September
Temperature 65°F; clear. Rainfall: nil.

11th Division (XVIII Corps)

A portion of the Divisional front was taken over by the 48th Division (XVIII Corps).

Sunday 30 September
Temperature 67°F; clear. Rainfall: nil.

3rd Division (II ANZAC Corps)

Relieved by the 3rd Australian Division (I ANZAC Corps).

23rd Division (X Corps)

At 5 a.m. the Germans counter-attacked under cover of smoke and flame-throwers. The attack was driven off by the 9th Yorks & Lancs (70th Brigade) north of the Menin Road.

5th Australian Division (II ANZAC Corps)

The Division were relieved by the 7th Division (X Corps).

Lancashire Fusiliers carrying duckboards over the mud near Pilckem, 10
October. (Q.6049)

OCTOBER

Monday 1 October

Temperature 69°F; clear. Rainfall: nil.

23rd Division (X Corps)

69 Brigade: At 5.30 a.m. a German attack was launched, supported by ground-attack aircraft, at the left of the Divisional front. The battalion on the left of the 9th Yorkshire Regiment fell back, causing the Yorks to fall back 150 yards to make a flank and link with the Leicestershire Regiment (110 Brigade, 21st Division). Three more attacks were driven off by rifle fire. The Germans dug in just east of an old line of their barbed wire, having gained 150 yards.

7th Division (X Corps)

22 Brigade: After a heavy barrage at 6.15 a.m. the Germans launched an attack on the 1st Royal Welsh Fusiliers, but it was driven off by artillery and small-arms fire. At 9 a.m. another attempt was made, with the same result. Later, German troops were seen concentrating in Cameron Covert and Joist Trench and were dispersed by artillery fire.

21st Division (X Corps)

110 Brigade: The 9th Leicesters[49] were on the right of the line and the 8th on the left. At 5 a.m. three strong infantry attacks were launched by the Germans on Glencorse Wood and Black Watch Corner in particular. One of these assaults forced the 9th Leicesters back from Joist Farm, but the line was re-established east of Cameron House.

4th and 5th Australian Divisions (I ANZAC Corps)

Parts of these divisions were relieved by the 1st Australian Division (I ANZAC Corps).

Tuesday 2 October

Temperature 76°F; showers. Rainfall: 2.7mm.

23rd Division (X Corps)

Relieved by the 5th Division (X Corps).

Wednesday 3 October

Temperature 64°F; overcast. Rainfall: 1.2mm.

5th Division (X Corps)

The Germans attacked 13 Brigade on the right but were repulsed.

37th Division (IX Corps)

The Germans attacked advanced posts on the Menin Road.

KOYLI personnel near Wieltje, on the way down from the trenches, 1 October. A gas gong is hanging from the tree on the right. (Q.6026)

Men of the KOYLI fusing Stokes trench mortar shells near Wieltje, 1 October. (Q.6025)

Thursday 4 October

Temperature 60°F; overcast. Rainfall: 4.6mm.

BATTLE OF BROODSEINDE

IX Corps
37th Division

63 Brigade attacked at 6 a.m. with the 8th Somerset Light Infantry[50], the 8th Lincolns, a company of the 10th Yorks & Lancs and two companies of the 4th Middlesex.

The right of the Somersets acted as anchor while the advance was made with the centre and left. They met with heavy small-arms fire but managed to take the Blue Line on the Tower Hamlets Spur. However, violent bombing counter-attacks forced the Somersets back to their start line. The Lincolns likewise came under heavy machine-gun fire from Joist Trench and Berry Cottage, forcing the attacking troops back to their start line. German counter-attacks from Joist

Trench were fought off and after dusk the line was straightened.

111 Brigade attacked with the 13th King's Royal Rifle Corps and the 13th Royal Fusiliers, supported by the 10th Royal Fusiliers. Attacking at 6 a.m., they came under fire from a blockhouse and Lewis Farm, which had been missed by the barrage. This hindered the Fusiliers as they performed a wheeling manoeuvre with the aim of taking the dug-outs strung out in the northern part of Gheluvelt Wood. As they wheeled they came under increased fire from Lewis Farm and the blockhouse and were forced to dig in short of their final objective.

The 13th KRRC advanced and occupied Tower Trench but were unable to hold it, being held up by machine-gun fire from their objective, Lewis Farm.

X Corps
5th Division

The Division attacked with two brigades. The German 19th Reserve Di-

vision were about to attack the 5th Division when the bombardment began and suffered many casualties as a consequence.

13 Brigade attacked with the 1st Royal West Kents and the 2nd King's Own Scottish Borderers. The right of the West Kents came under fire from a pillbox south of the Menin Road and located in the 37th Division area (probably Lewis Farm). The West Kents were forced to adopt a defensive front facing the pillbox. The centre and left kept pace with the KOSB and held the ground taken. At 12.30 p.m. they reported that the objective had been consolidated and that they were in touch with the KOSB.

The KOSB flanked the Reutelbeek to the north and the Scherriabeek to the south in their attack on Polderhoek Château. They advanced some 700 yards to the edge of the grounds of the château but could go no further. One tank managed to keep up with the advance and helped with the attack. This position was then consolidated.

95 Brigade attacked with the 1st Devons and the 1st Duke of Cornwall's Light Infantry; the 1st East Surreys were in support and the 12th Gloucesters in reserve. The Cornwalls almost immediately came under fire from the western edge of the wood, known as Cameron Covert. Scattered pillboxes in the area also checked the advance for a short time.

Stiff fighting took place in Cameron Copse until the Germans were driven out. The infantry were helped by three tanks that were going down the Reutel road. The advance continued to the final objective, Juniper Hill, which proved to be untenable as it was enfiladed by machine-gun and artillery

[49]VC: T/Lt-Col Philip Eric Bent, Commander.
[50]VC: Pte Thomas Henry Sage.

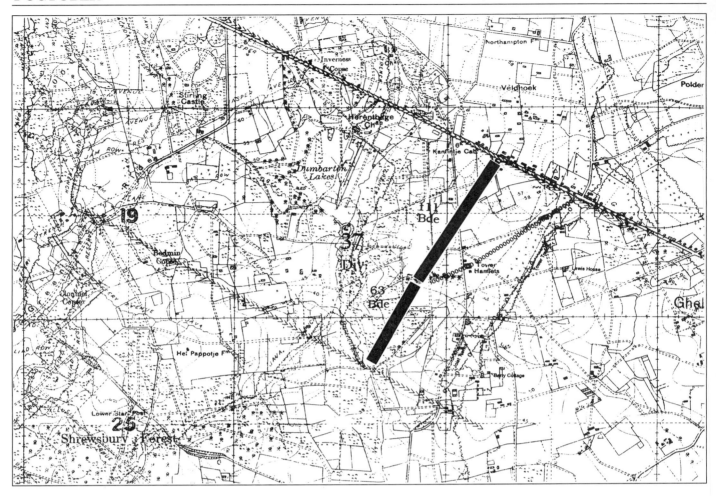

fire. However, the attackers moved to the north of the Reutel road and linked up with troops of the 21st Division on their left.

Around 7 p.m. it was found that there was a gap between the Cornwalls and the Devons. It was filled by the East Surreys coming up from the neighbourhood of Cameron House.

The Germans launched eight counter-attacks and regained the ground they had lost on the Polderhoek Spur. At nightfall the front ran along the west side of Cameron Covert and just west of Château Wood.

21st Division[51]
The Division attacked at 6 a.m. with two brigades.
64 Brigade attacked with the 9th King's Own Yorkshire Light Infantry; the 10th KOYLI were in support. The 9th KOYLI advanced under heavy ma-

chine-gun fire. After taking Joist Farm with some difficulty, they were confronted with a marsh lined with concrete forts to the right. These were attacked by bombers. Juniper Trench was cut off and captured while three more blockhouses were attacked successfully and the objective was reached. They came under fire from a strongpoint on the east of Reutel, but this was put out of action by a tank. The 9th KOYLI consolidated and the right of the Battalion was forced to make a defensive flank.

Around noon a counter-attack was launched from the south-east but was beaten off by artillery and small-arms fire.
62 Brigade attacked with the 3/4th Queen's[52] advancing across the Polygonebeek and adjacent marsh. Juniper Trench was carried, along with a blockhouse. The attack continued to

Judge Trench and consolidation was begun.

The attack was taken up by the 1st Lincolnshire Regiment[53]. They suffered casualties from fire from the area of Judge Copse to the east but managed to consolidate their position. Later they were shelled, but no counter-attack took place.

7th Division
The Division attacked at 6 a.m., zero hour, with two brigades.
91 Brigade: The 1st South Staffs encountered little resistance and waited on the Red Line. In advancing to the Blue Line, they came under fire from the right (21st Divisional area), but when the Queen's (21st Division) caught up, things were secure. The 22nd Manchesters advanced with their left making for In Der Star Cabaret and they came under machine-gun fire

from Joiner's Rest and were held up. The 21st Manchesters reinforced them with three companies and together they consolidated the Blue Line. At noon they were ordered to form a defensive flank on their right and the 2nd Queen's (22 Brigade) were sent up to help. Two companies were deployed along Jolting Houses road, facing south, and a company in Jetty Trench. Touch was gained with the 21st Division's left west of Reutel.

20 Brigade attacked with the 8th Devons, who encountered little opposition and reached the Red Line in good time. The 2nd Gordon Highlanders took over the attack but strayed over to the left in tandem with the Australians on their left. Consequently the 2nd Borderers had to spread themselves to cover the gap. However, they met with little opposition and the final objective was taken and consolidated.

I ANZAC Corps
1st Australian Division
The Division attacked at 5.25 a.m., zero hour, with two brigades.

1 Australian Brigade: The 3rd Battalion, despite meeting pockets of opposition, went well but overshot the Red Line. They were brought back and consolidated the position. At 8.10 a.m. the 1st and 4th Battalions went forward and, although they pulled to the left, stayed in touch with the troops on their flanks. The commanding officer decided to prepare for counter-attacks and leave re-adjustment to later. They dug in, with the 1st Battalion in old trenches and the 4th partly behind some German wire.

2 Australian Brigade: The 8th Battalion advanced through the marsh and tree stumps of Romulus and Remus Woods north of Molenaarelsthoek and came under fire from a nest of pillboxes. These were ultimately outflanked. Parties of the 8th Battalion were forced into the area of the 2nd Australian Division. They arrived at the first ob-

jective at 7.15 a.m. and for better observation consolidated 100 yards in advance of the Red Line. Whilst doing so they came under fire from four 77mm guns in a position on the Becelaere≈Broodseinde road. An officer and a few men attacked and captured the guns.

The 6th and 7th Battalions took over the attack. The 6th lost direction and crowded the 7th. However, they maintained touch with both flanks. Both battalions came under heavy fire from Retaliation Farm and also a large crater[54] used as a German headquarters and strongpoint. This was taken by the 6th Battalion. They carried on the advance and came under fire from the distant Keiberg position. The Blue Line was consolidated and posts were established 75 yards in front of the line.

No counter-attacks were launched, but the enemy were seen massing at 12 noon at Dame House and Celtic Wood, at 1 p.m. and 2.30 p.m. at Flint Farm and twice near Keiberg. Artillery fire dispersed the enemy.

2nd Australian Division
The Division attacked at 5.25 a.m., zero hour, with two brigades, met the same German counter-attacks as the 1st Australian Division and likewise fought them off.

6 Australian Brigade: Chasing the retreating Germans, the Brigade skirted Zonnebeke Lake and helped capture the village itself. On the way they captured four anti-tank field guns and carried on over their first objective without stopping, although some companies were brought back to the first objective. The final objective was taken, including Broodseinde village.

7 Australian Brigade cleared Zonnebeke village of snipers etc and continued on their way, only to encounter severe fire from German machine guns in Daisy Wood, some 300 yards away, as they reached the top of the ridge. It was decided to consolidate along a well-

placed old British trench from 1914–15, 200 yards short of their objective.

II ANZAC Corps
3rd Australian Division[55]
The Division attacked at 5.25 a.m., zero hour, with two brigades.

11 Australian Brigade attacked with the 44th Battalion; the 41st Battalion were in support. They were held up by the Seine strongpoint but this was rushed by parts of the 41st, who went on to the final objective and dug in.

10 Australian Brigade attacked with the 39th Battalion. They were held up by machine-gun fire from pillboxes in the New Zealand Division's area, but these were dealt with by the 40th Battalion[56] who were in support. They went on and were forced to storm Hamburg and consolidate.

New Zealand Division
The Division attacked at 5.25 a.m., zero hour, with two brigades. In their advance to the Red Line the New Zealanders had to cross the Hanebeek. Like the Australians, they were also to be the target of a German counter-attack, but the opening barrage took care of most of the enemy.

4 NZ Brigade: The advance started on time with the 3rd Auckland and the 3rd Otago. They took Dochy Farm and Riverside in their stride. Otto Farm put up more resistance but also fell, and the Brigade moved on to the Red Line, which they consolidated.

The attack was taken over by the 3rd Canterbury and the 3rd Wellington. The Canterburys were held up temporarily by two pillboxes in Berlin Wood and the Wellingtons were caught by two pillboxes not shown on their

---

[51]VC: A/Capt Clement Robertson.
[52]This was an amalgamated battalion, not Territorial.
[53]VC: A/Lt-Col Lewis Pugh Evans, Commander.
[54]Believed to be the result of an ammunition dump which had exploded.
[55]VC: L-Cpl Walter Peeler.
[56]VC: Sgt Lewis McGee.

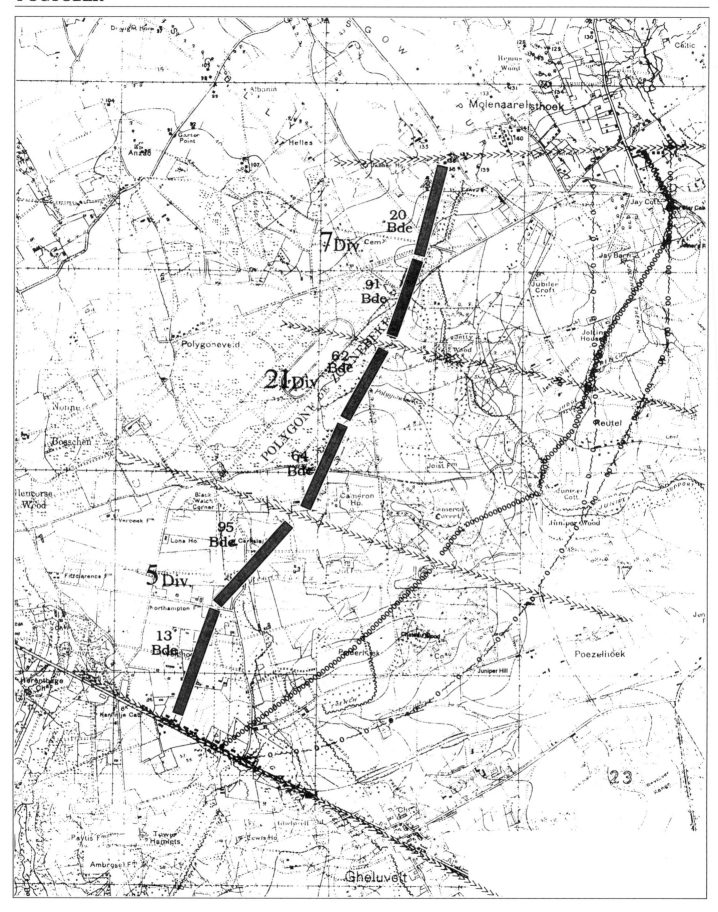

map. These they took before going on to attack the farm known as Berlin, which they consolidated.

1 NZ Brigade attacked with the 1st Auckland and the 1st Wellington. The Aucklanders drifted to the north, dragging the northern companies of the Wellingtons with them, and came under fire immediately from pillboxes around Aviatik Farm and Dear House; these were cleared with bomb and trench-mortar fire. On their extreme left, in the 48th Division's front, they came under fire from Winzig, Albatross Farm and Winchester, all of which they took and consolidated.

The Wellingtons came under fire from Boetleer pillboxes. These were cleared and the Wellingtons carried on to the Red Line. On reaching the crest they came under fire from two dugouts in front of Korek. These were about 120 yards beyond the objective and, under the British barrage, were cleared by troops from the Wellingtons and the 3rd Otago (4 NZ Brigade).

The 2nd Auckland and the 2nd Wellington took up the advance from the Red Line and, working together, captured a German battalion headquarters in the group of pillboxes known as Waterloo. The Aucklanders went on through the brick ruins of Korek to Calgary Grange. The Wellingtons met resistance from Kronprinz Farm but went on to consolidate the final position.

XVIII Corps
48th Division

The Division attacked with one brigade at 6 a.m., zero hour. On the right, the 1/5th Warwicks captured Vale House, followed soon afterwards by Winzig. They came under heavy fire from a machine-gun post and the left company took severe casualties. The New Zealanders, on the right, moved across the front of the 1/5th and took up a line between Albatross Farm and Wellington, causing much confusion.

This was not corrected until the 1/6th Warwicks had taken Winchester Farm and the New Zealanders Albatross Farm, allowing the 1/5th to move on to the Stroombeek. At dusk they took over the line of the New Zealanders and advanced it a little.

In the centre the 1/6th Warwicks took some posts along the west bank of the Stroombeek. Continuing the advance, they came under heavy fire from the high ground and road in front of York Farm. The fighting became confused and it was some time before Winchester was taken. Eventually a line 300 yards west of Vacher Farm was taken. At 1 p.m. two companies of the 1/8th Warwicks were sent up to capture the final objective, but fire was too heavy for much progress to be made.

The 1/7th Warwicks[57], on the left, came under machine-gun fire from the start. Tweed House was taken, however, and touch was gained with the troops on the left. The left of the 1/7th reached Beek House while the right advanced 50 yards to the west of the cemetery but were forced back.

At 5 p.m. the attack was to continue with the 5th Gloucesters and the 4th Ox & Bucks, but a heavy rainstorm and darkness prevented any further advance.

11th Division

The Division attacked at 6 a.m., zero hour, with two brigades and ten tanks of 'D' Battalion (1st Tank Brigade). *34 Brigade* attacked with the 9th Lancashire Fusiliers and the 11th Manchesters[58]; the 5th Dorsets were in support. After neutralizing Malta House with Stokes mortar fire, the 9th Lancs moved to the Red Dotted Line. A feeble counter-attack was launched at the Manchesters but was driven off by small-arms fire. The Red Line fell with little trouble.

The Manchesters were held up for a while by fire from the direction of the

church and the Brewery in Poelcapelle. Gloster Farm was taken with the help of a trench mortar and two tanks. The Red Line was consolidated.

Poelcapelle was entered by units of both brigades. The tanks hunted the enemy down and captured the garrisons of several pillboxes beyond the eastern exit.

33 Brigade attacked with the 7th South Staffordshire Regiment and the 9th Sherwood Foresters[59]; the 6th Border Regiment were in reserve. There was no serious opposition to the advance to the Red Dotted Line. The South Staffs passed by a derelict tank that was found to have a German machine-gun post hidden underneath. In the advance to the Red Line they encountered and dealt with small parties of the enemy in shell holes. A concrete shelter was taken near Poelcapelle Church. Consolidation was hampered by snipers in the village.

As they advanced, the Foresters cleared Ferdan House and moved on to the Red Line, meeting little opposition. The division on the left fell back 400 yards, forcing the Foresters to maintain a flank until they regained their position.

The Germans counter-attacked at 1 p.m. but were driven off. The 5th Dorsets and the 6th Borderers were brought up to support the attack and dug in between the Steenbeek and the Langemarck≈Winnipeg road.

XIV Corps
4th Division

11 Brigade attacked at 6 a.m., zero hour, with the 1st Somerset Light Infantry and the 1st Hampshire Regiment; the 1st East Lancashire Regiment were in support and the 1st Rifle Brigade in reserve. Assaulted at 6 a.m., Kangaroo Trench was taken with little trouble. On reaching the road which

---

[57]VC: Pte Arthur Hunt.
[58]VC: Sgt Charles Harry Coverdale.
[59]VC: A/Cpl Fred Greaves.

was the first objective, the Brigade were held up by Germans sheltering behind several rock piles. These were cleared by small-arms fire. Fire from Lemnos House also held up the attack for a while before being dealt with.

On the right of the Somersets the Brigade joined with the 11th Division and successfully attacked a pillbox on the Poelcapelle road. On progressing to the Green Line, the Somersets combined with the East Lancs and outflanked Ferdan House, which had been causing problems. They came under machine-gun fire from 19 Metre Hill whilst consolidating the Green Line. *10 Brigade*, attacking at 6 a.m. with the 2nd Seaforth Highlanders and with the 3/10th Middlesex in support, crossed the Laudetbeek Marsh and lost direction. The Brigade came under machine-gun fire from its left flank. The Seaforths, reinforced by some Middlesex, achieved their first objective, a line on the road on the far side of 19 Metre Hill. After pausing for an hour they continued the attack but, still under machine-gun fire, abandoned it and consolidated.

At 3 p.m. the Germans counter-attacked and came to within 80 yards of the Brigade's position but were driven back when the 1st East Lancs (11 Brigade) and the 1st Royal Warwicks came to assist. A gap between the 4th and the 29th Divisions on the left was filled at nightfall by two companies of the 1st Warwicks. At 5 p.m. the enemy were seen massing for another attack but were scattered by artillery fire.

The line held at the end of the day was as follows: Ferdan House–Kangaroo Huts–west of Tragique Farm–19 Metre Hill. Touch was made with troops on both flanks.

29th Division

The Division was to form a defensive flank overlooking the Broembeek valley. They attacked at 6 a.m., zero hour. *86 Brigade*, advancing with two platoons of the 1st King's Own Scottish Borderers, successfully attacked three blockhouses on and near the railway.

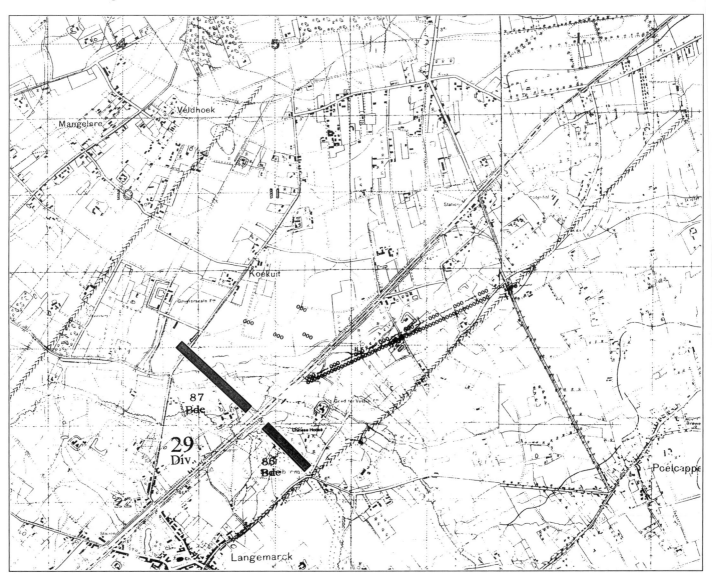

87 *Brigade* attacked with the 1st Royal Dublin Fusiliers[60], whose task was to form a flank with the 4th Division. The Dubliners succeeded in their task, taking Chinese House and 't Goed ter Vesten Farm on the way.

The Germans counter-attacked the 4th Division, who were driven back. The 29th Division then enfiladed the attacking Germans, who in turn fell back, and the 4th Division regained their lost ground.

Friday 5 October

Temperature 52°F; 50% cloud cover, showers. Rainfall: 3.1mm.

21st Division (X Corps)
64 Brigade: The 15th Durham Light Infantry attacked and captured a blockhouse.

3rd Australian Division (II ANZAC Corps)
Relieved by the 66th Division (II ANZAC Corps).

New Zealand Division (II ANZAC Corps)
Relieved by 49th Division (II ANZAC Corps).

Saturday 6 October

Temperature 47°F; 50% cloud cover. Rainfall: 2.1mm.

2nd Australian Division (I ANZAC Corps)
Daisy Wood was reported to be strongly held by Germans.

The Battle of Poelcappelle: men of the 4th Battalion The Coldstream Guards sit on a 150mm gun—known to the British as a 5.9-inch—outside a German concrete blockhouse on the outskirts of Houthulst Forest during the attack of 9 October. (Q.6046)

Sunday 7 October

Temperature 53°F; cloud cover. Rainfall: 10.4mm.

48th Division (XVIII Corps)
143 Brigade: An attack on Burns House and Vacher Farm failed.

49th Division (II ANZAC Corps)
Parties of the 11th and 12th Battalions raided Celtic Wood.

Monday 8 October

Temperature 54°F; overcast with showers. Rainfall: 14.6mm.

14th Division (II Corps)
The Division was relieved by the 33rd Division (X Corps).

Tuesday 9 October

Temperature 53°F; clear. Rainfall: nil.

23rd Division (X Corps)
Relieved by the 7th Division (X Corps).

1st Australian Division (I ANZAC Corps)
The 10th Battalion raided Celtic Wood.

BATTLE OF POELCAPELLE (9 October)

SECOND ARMY
X Corps
5th Division
The Division attacked with one brigade (13 Brigade, on the right of 15 Brigade, were in the line but did not attack).
15 Brigade attacked with the 1st Norfolks and the 16th Warwicks. Moving forward at 5.20 a.m., they were checked by fire from Polderhoek Château and supporting pillboxes. Fire and the mud stopped any real progress being made and the troops were forced back to their original position. Another attack scheduled for that night was cancelled.

21st Division
The 21st Division, between the 5th and the 7th Divisions, did not attack.

[60]VC: Sgt James Ockenden.

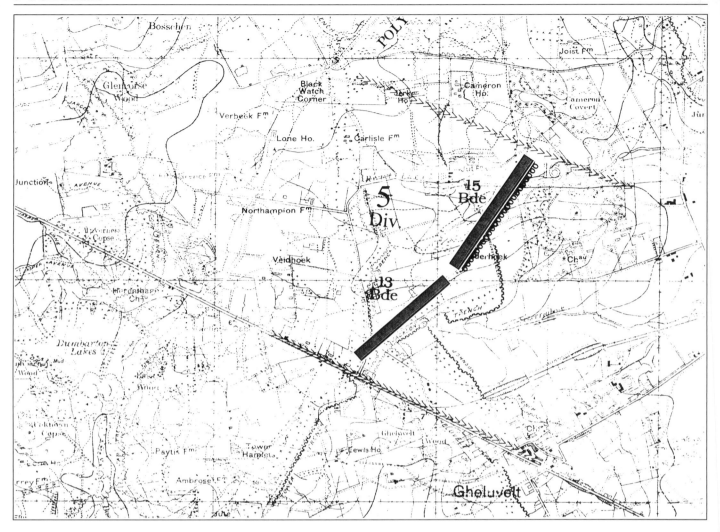

7th Division

The Division attacked with one brigade.

22 Brigade attacked at 5.20 a.m. with the 2nd Honourable Artillery Company and the 2nd Royal Warwickshires; the 9th Devons were in reserve. The HAC took Reutel and cleared part of the cemetery east of the village but were held up short of Juniper Cottage by machine-gun fire. The Warwickshires passed through Judge Copse but failed to complete the mopping up. At dusk, after several attempts, the copse fell to the Devons and the gains were secured.

I ANZAC Corps
2nd Australian Division

The Division's task was to cover the right flank of the 66th Division and it attacked with 5 Australian Brigade at 5.20 a.m., zero hour, while 6 Brigade formed a flank.

6 Australian Brigade attacked with the 22nd, 24th, 21st and 23rd Battalions, which had an average strength of seven officers and 150 other ranks. The 22nd attacked and took the sand pit on the Moorslede road. The 24th advanced the 200 yards to Daisy Wood in spite of coming under fire from the wood and also Dairy Wood 150 yards further north. The 21st should have passed between the two woods but was held up before reaching them, but posts were dug and they were in touch with the 23rd on their left. The 23rd veered northwards and came in behind the 17th (5 Australian Brigade), missing Dairy Wood. As they advanced they dropped off posts to guard the flank ending at Rhine, a fortified farm ruin on the Brigade's left, thereby guarding the flank of 5 Brigade.

5 Australian Brigade attacked with the 20th Battalion and with the 17th in support. They came under enfilade fire from a machine-gun across the railway in the 66th Divisional area. By this time the two battalions were intermixed. They went on to the first objective, taking on the way a strongpost made of old cement bags near Defy Crossing. They waited in front of Keiberg whilst the barrage played on the pillboxes. Decoy Wood was cleared, as was Rhine. On the left the railway cutting was cleared with bomb and bayonet. They reached the final objective, but with so few men remaining they were forced back to the first objective, which they consolidated.

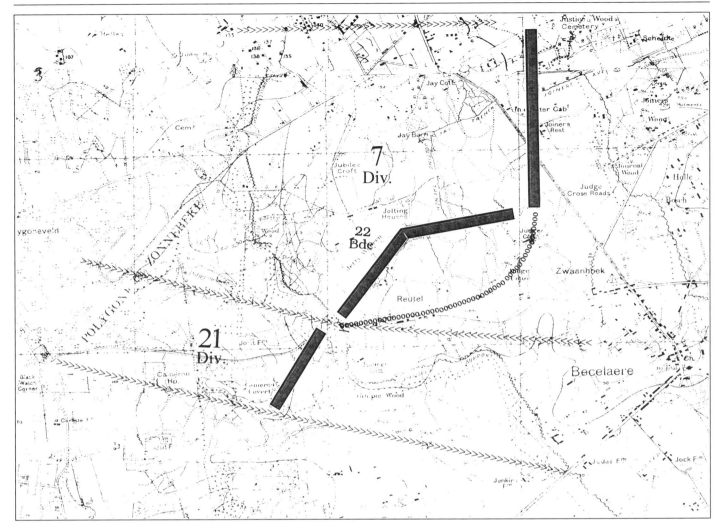

II ANZAC Corps
66th Division

The Division attacked at 5.20 a.m., zero hour, with two brigades.

198 Brigade attacked with the 2/9th Manchesters and the 2/4th East Lancs; the 2/5th East Lancs were in support and the 2/10th Manchesters in reserve. The assaulting troops immediately came under severe artillery and machine-gun fire. The 2/5th East Lancs came under heavy fire from Hamburg Redoubt, which they attacked without success.

By midday it became apparent that the Brigade had only reached the first objective. Consolidation was begun. The remnants of the 2/5th were pulled back to form a line behind the two front-line battalions in anticipation of counter-attacks.

At dusk the enemy launched a counter-attack, which was repulsed by artillery and small-arms fire, the 2/5th East Lancs being usefully employed.

197 Brigade, comprising four battalions of the Lancashire Fusiliers, attacked with the 3/5th Lancashire Fusiliers. The attack was then taken over by the 2/6th and 2/8th, with the 2/7th in reserve. The Brigade advanced in dribs and drabs owing to the state of the ground.

The 3/5th Lancashire Fusiliers advanced with their right on the Roulers railway and took the Red Line. They linked with the 2/6th at about 9.30 a.m. and joined 198 Brigade in Augustus Wood on the right.

Meanwhile the 2/8th and part of the 3/5th were pushing on towards the Blue Line, which they reached by 9.30 a.m. and started to consolidate. Patrols were sent out and some reached the outskirts of Passchendaele itself.[61]

The Germans launched two counter-attacks in the morning but were driven off with small-arms fire. A defensive flank was formed on the left but troops of the 66th Division, seeing the defensive withdrawal, mistook it for a general withdrawal and they fell back to the Red Line at about 1.30 p.m.

The Red Line was firmly held by the 3/5th, 2/8th and 2/6th Lancs. Orders were received to retake the Blue Line but they were later abandoned.

The Division was in touch with the 2nd Australian Division and the 49th Division on their flanks.

---

[61]Bodies of the men from these two battalions were found when the village fell on 6 November.

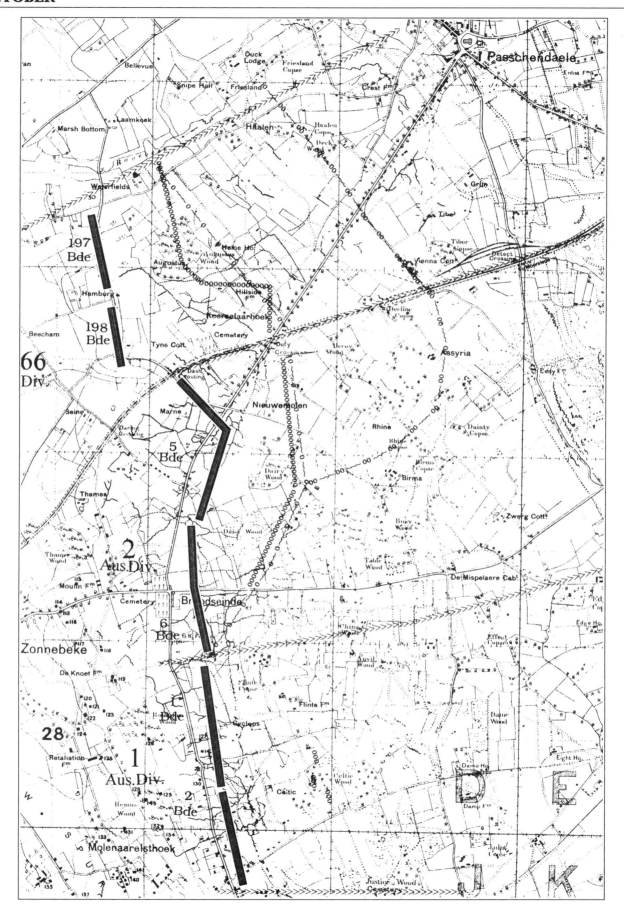

49th Division

148 Brigade attacked at 5.20 a.m., zero hour, with the 4th and 5th Yorks & Lancs and the 5th King's Own Yorkshire Light Infantry in the first line, leaving the 4th KOYLI in reserve. They came across the Ravebeek—now some 30 to 50 yards wide and waist deep at its midpoint—which forced them to close on the Meetcheele–Gravenstafel road. The left came under fire from machine guns and rifles and the right was held up in the morass. The 4th KOYLI were sent up to reinforce the attack.

The whole Brigade was now in one line. They advanced up a long slope and came under fire from Wolf Copse on the left and Bellevue on the top of the slope. Casualties forced the troops to dig in along the slope. At 7 p.m. an attempt was made to take the two pillboxes on the ridge but they were so heavily wired that the attack had to be abandoned.

146 Brigade attacked with the 1/5th, 1/7th and 1/8th West Yorkshire Regiment in line and the 1/6th in reserve. The 1/5th finally reached a line 200 yards in front of the Red Line, and a support line was established on the Red Line. The 1/7th advanced and took Yetta House and the pillbox Peter Pan; the line finished up near Peter Pan and in touch with the 1/5th. The 1/8th only managed to advance 300 yards and dug in around Kronprinz Farm, which was used as a Battalion

Right, top: Royal Engineers taking telephone wire up to the front between Pilckem and Langemarck, 10 October. The man on left is wearing a Signaller's brassard. (Q.6050)

Right, centre: A fatigue party of Irish Guards taking up duckboards near Langemarck, 10 October. (Q.6053)

Right, bottom: Batteries on Anzac Ridge crowd their guns until they are almost touching each other. 1st Division, 2nd Brigade AFA, 10 October. (E[AUS].4645)

HQ. They held this position tenaciously until 10 October.

A gap had developed between the two Brigades and the 1/6th were sent to fill it. They went to the vicinity of Peter Pan and consolidated 150 yards west of it. During the night touch was gained with the 1/5th Lancashire Fusiliers and the 1/4th Yorks & Lancs (148th Brigade).

FIFTH ARMY
XVIII Corps
48th Division
The Division attacked at 5.20 a.m., zero hour, with one brigade.

114 Brigade attacked with the 7th Worcesters and the 4th and 6th Gloucesters; the 8th Worcesters were in reserve. It came under machine-gun fire from the start, allowing the barrage to get away from the troops.

The 4th Gloucesters, facing fire from Oxford House and Berks Houses, were held up 150 yards east of County Crossroads, while the 7th Worcesters attacked Adler Farm and took the trenches in front of it. Two companies unsuccessfully attacked Inch Farm. The 6th Gloucesters cleared the cemetery and the advance carried on beyond Vacher Farm; Adler Farm was taken.

At 2.45 p.m. a company of 8th Worcesters made another attack on Inch Farm, but it came under fire from British guns as a barrage was put down to protect the 6th Gloucesters from a German counter-attack. At 5 p.m. another company of the 8th Worcesters tried but failed to take Oxford House.

11th Division
The Division attacked with one brigade.

33 Brigade attacked at 5.20 a.m. with the 6th Green Howards (32 Brigade[62]) and the 9th West Yorkshire Regiment. Advancing to the left of Poelcapelle village, the Green Howards initially met little resistance in the village, but on nearing the fork in the road opposite the Brewery they came under fire from Meunier House and from the direction of Stirling House. They cleared a number of pillboxes northwest of the Brewery. These could not be held, and a line was established a short distance in the rear. At 11.15 a.m. the 8th Duke of Wellington's were brought up in close support.

The West Yorks encountered enfilade fire from the village and took severe casualties. Seeing the Green Howards pulling back, they too fell back and eventually established a line near their assembly position. The 6th

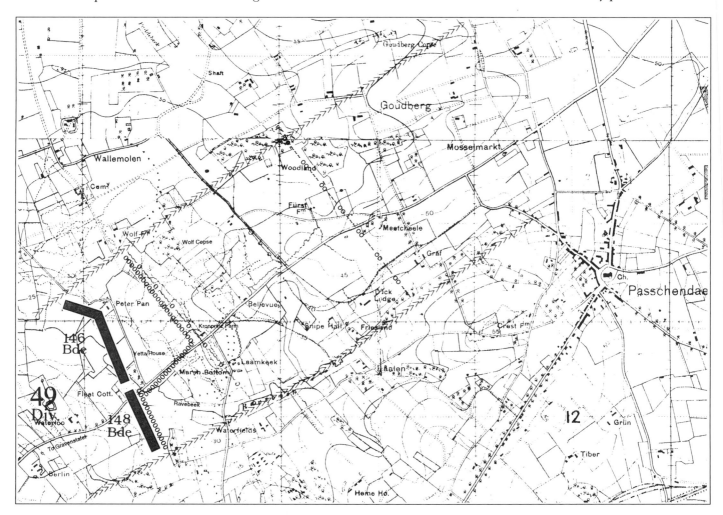

Lincolns were brought up in line between Pheasant Farm and Retour crossroads.

XIV Corps
4th Division

The Division attacked with one brigade.

12 Brigade attacked at 5.20 a.m. with the 2nd Essex and the 2nd Lancashire Fusiliers; the 2nd Duke of Wellington's were in support and the 1st King's Own (R Lancs) in reserve.

The first objective was reached at 5.45 a.m. and taken. The left of the attack then came under fire from blockhouses to the north-east of Poelcapelle, which had not been taken by the 11th Division. The Lancashire Fusiliers came under small-arms fire from near Landing Farm, Compromise Farm north of Poelcapelle and Millers Farm

on the Divisional boundary. Millers Farm was dealt with, progress resumed and a gap of 200 yards opened between them and the 11th Division. They reached and consolidated a position half way between the first and second objectives, advancing 400 yards on the right and 600 on the left.

29th Division

The Division attacked with two brigades.

86 Brigade attacked at 5.20 a.m. The 1st Lancashire Fusiliers[63] came under fire from Olga House, which was cleared. It was something of a mixed party as the 2nd Royal Fusiliers[64], in support, had become mixed up with the Lancs, who had reached the Green Dotted Line and linked up with the 2nd Lancashire Fusiliers (4th Division) on the right near Millers Farm.

Just as the advance was to continue, a German counter-attack was launched but this was beaten off by small-arms fire. The attack proceeded and the Blue Line was reached and Senegal Farm occupied. Here a flank guard was established; this was soon tested by another German counter-attack, but it held. A line of posts was established from Tranquille House to Senegal Farm along the final objective.

88 Brigade attacked with the 4th Worcesters[65] and met strong opposition from pillboxes along the railway embankment. These were dealt with. The Royal Newfoundland Regiment, in support, had become intermixed with the Worcesters and both units arrived

[62]VC: Cpl William Clamp.
[63]VC: Sgt Joseph Lister.
[64]VC: Sgt John Molyneaux.
[65]VC: Pte Frederick George Dancox.

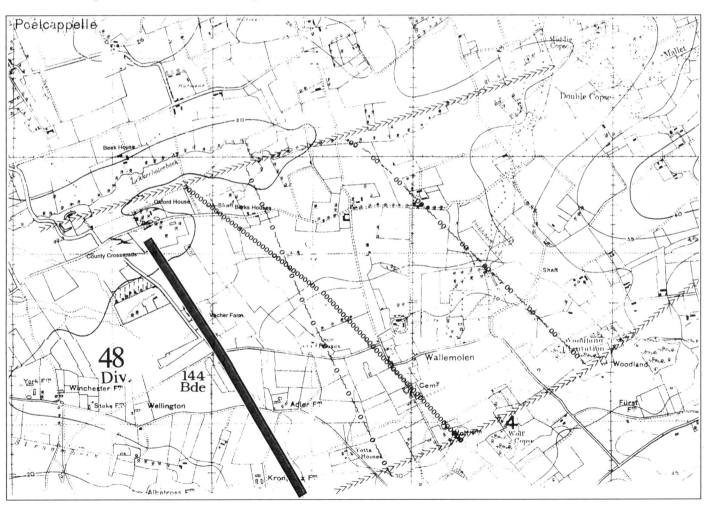

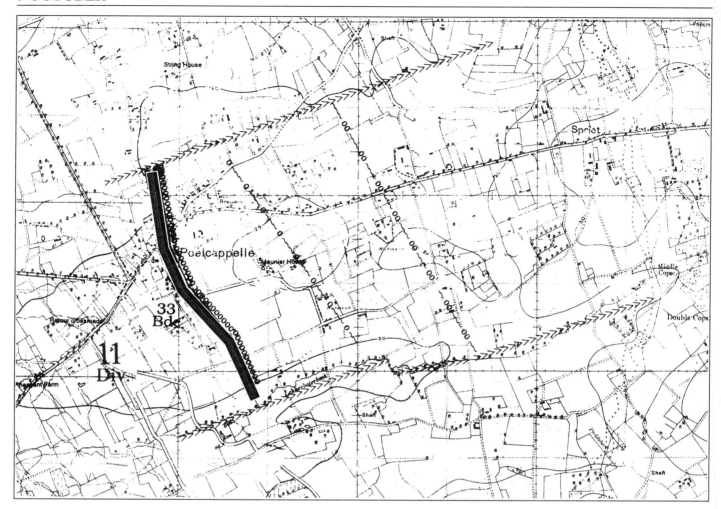

Left: The Butt, a well-known point in Polygon Wood, 11 October. Around its slopes are thickly strewn the shell-torn bodies of more than a hundred German, Australian and English troops. (E[AUS].987)

Above: The remains of a line of German strongpoints near St Julien, 12 October. (Q.6060)

at the first objective, Namur Crossing (where a road ran under the railway embankment). The consolidating men came under fire from a blockhouse in front of their position which had not been cleared, but before mortars could be brought up it was single-handedly captured.[66]

On the way to the second objective a blockhouse 300 yards to the front, near the railway and Pascal Farm, caused some casualties but was dealt with by trench mortar fire. By 9 a.m.

the second objective had been taken. The Newfoundlanders passed through and went on to take Cairo House and the line of the third objective.

Guards Division

The Division attacked at 5.20 a.m., zero hour, with two brigades.
1 Guards Brigade attacked with the 2nd Grenadiers and the 2nd Coldstreams. Having waded across a stream, they re-formed on the far bank and went on to take the first objective by 6 a.m., meeting little opposition.

The blockhouse near Vee Bend offered some resistance but surrendered when outflanked. The Brigade went on to the second objective and consolidated. The 1st Irish Guards passed through and came under fire from Egypt Farm and the Brickfield, which was defended stoutly. This fell, and

they went on to take their final objective but were forced to throw back a defensive flank, bent back eastward from Angle Point, as the Newfoundlanders (29th Division) on their right had not caught up.

A German counter-attack was launched that evening on the 29th Division, which fell back a little, forcing the 1st Irish Guards to pull back. *2 Guards Brigade*[67] crossed the Broembeek (the banks of which were little better than a swamp) by bridges. Despite machine-gun fire from Ney Wood which held up the 2nd Irish Guards for a while, the first objective was taken. By 8.15 a.m. the second objective was taken without organized opposition having been met.

---

[66] By Pte Dancox.
[67] VC: L-Sgt John Harold Rhodes.

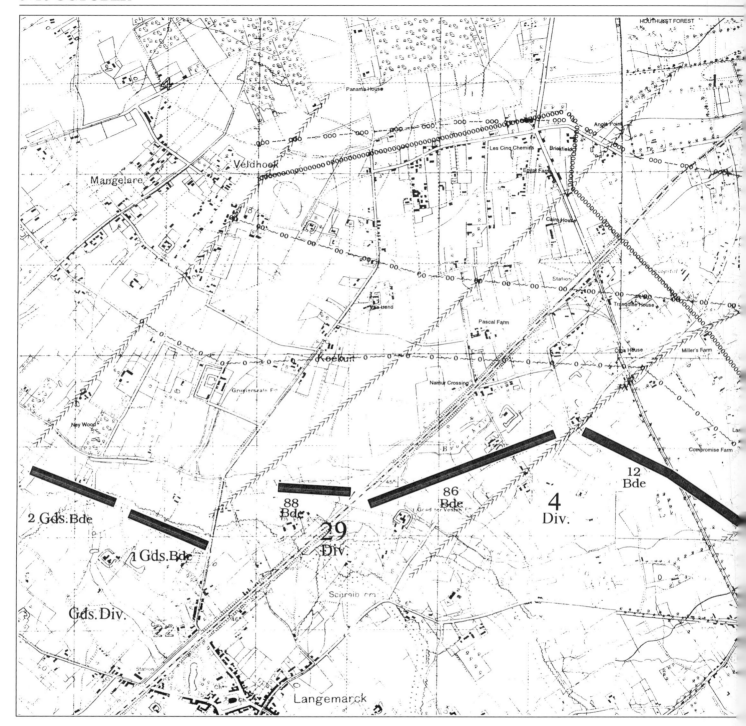

The 3rd Coldstreams, taking over the attack, encountered fierce rifle fire from Houthulst Forest and Les Cinq Chemins. This was stemmed, however, and the third objective was taken and consolidated. The 1st Coldstreams came under heavy fire from a German strongpoint on the left, but they decided to skirt this and press on to the final objective. This they reached at about the same time as the others, and at 1.30 p.m. the 1st Coldsteams cleared the strongpoint that had been passed by.

The Germans started to mass around Panama House but were dispersed by machine-gun fire. Two German counter-attacks launched at the junction between the Guards and the French were stopped by artillery fire.

Wednesday 10 October

Temperature 48°F; 25% cloud cover with showers. Rainfall: 2.5mm

11th Division (XVIII Corps)
Relieved by the 18th Division (XVIII Corps).

48th Division (XVIII Corps)
Relieved by the 9th Division (V Corps).

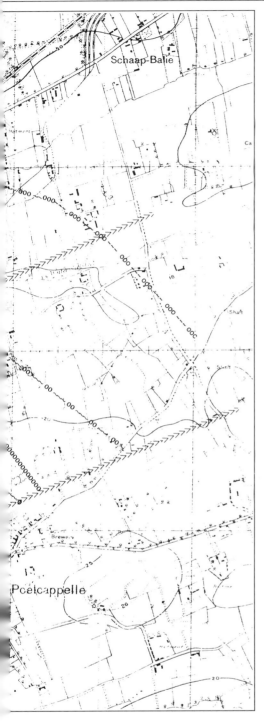

Schaap-Balie

Poelcappelle

66th Division (II ANZAC Corps)
The Division repulsed a counter-attack, and during the night was relieved by the 3rd Australian Division (II ANZAC Corps).

1st Australian Division (I ANZAC Corps)
Relieved by the 5th Australian Division (I ANZAC Corps).

Thursday 11 October
Temperature 50°F; 50% cloud cover with showers. Rainfall: 4.9mm.

29th Division (XIV Corps)
Relieved by the 17th Division (XIV Corps).

49th Division (II ANZAC Corps)
Relieved by the New Zealand Division (II ANZAC Corps).

2nd Australian Division (I ANZAC Corps)
Relieved by the 4th Australian Division (I ANZAC Corps).

5th Division (X Corps)
Relieved by the 14th Division (X Corps).

Friday 12 October
Temperature 55°F; rain. Rainfall: 7.9mm.

36th Division (XIX Corps)
The Germans launched a dummy raid on the left front of the Division.

FIRST BATTLE OF PASSCHENDAELE (12 October)

I ANZAC Corps
4th Australian Division
The Division was flank guard to the 3rd Australian Division.
12 Australian Brigade were to protect the flank of the main attack with outposts across the Keiberg Spur. Two battalions, the 47th and the 48th, were used and their task was to take the Red and Blue Lines respectively.

The battalions set off at 5.20 a.m., zero hour, and the Red Line, with the exception of a portion near Assyria, was reached on time by the 47th and was consolidated. The 48th Battalion passed through and, while waiting for

the barrage, gained touch with the 3rd Australian Division at a point on the railway. Here they were told that the 3rd Australian would not carry on their advance. The 48th Battalion came under fire from Vienna Cottage. Assyria was taken with the aid of two Stokes mortars. As the 47th could no longer advance, the 48th decided they would consolidate the position held. This was achieved with difficulty and great loss. Two German counter-attacks were launched, one at 4 p.m. and another at 5 p.m; both were driven off by small-arms fire—but to no avail, as the positions had to be abandoned on the withdrawal of 9 Brigade (3rd Australian Division).

II ANZAC Corps
3rd Australian Division
The Division attacked with two brigades at 5.25 a.m., 350 yards behind the general line of attack.
9 Australian Brigade advanced in total confusion with the 34th Battalion[68] because of heavy shelling on the jump-off line. The 35th Battalion, in support, overran Defy Crossing, Hillside Farm and Augustus Wood machine-gun posts on the way to its first objective. It pressed on astride the Passchendaele road to the second objective in front of Passchendaele village, where wounded of the 66th Division from the attack on 9 September were found still hiding in shell holes. Patrols entered the village and found it abandoned, but the attack was not strong enough to secure it and soon after 3 p.m. they too were forced to retire almost back to their start line.
10 Australian Brigade attacked south of the Ravebeek with the 37th, 38th and 40th Battalions and came under fire from Augustus Wood and Waterfields in the Ravebeek bog on the left. Waterfields fell to the 40th Battalion, which was stopped at its first objective by enfilade machine-gun fire across

[68]VC: Capt Clarence Smith Jeffries.

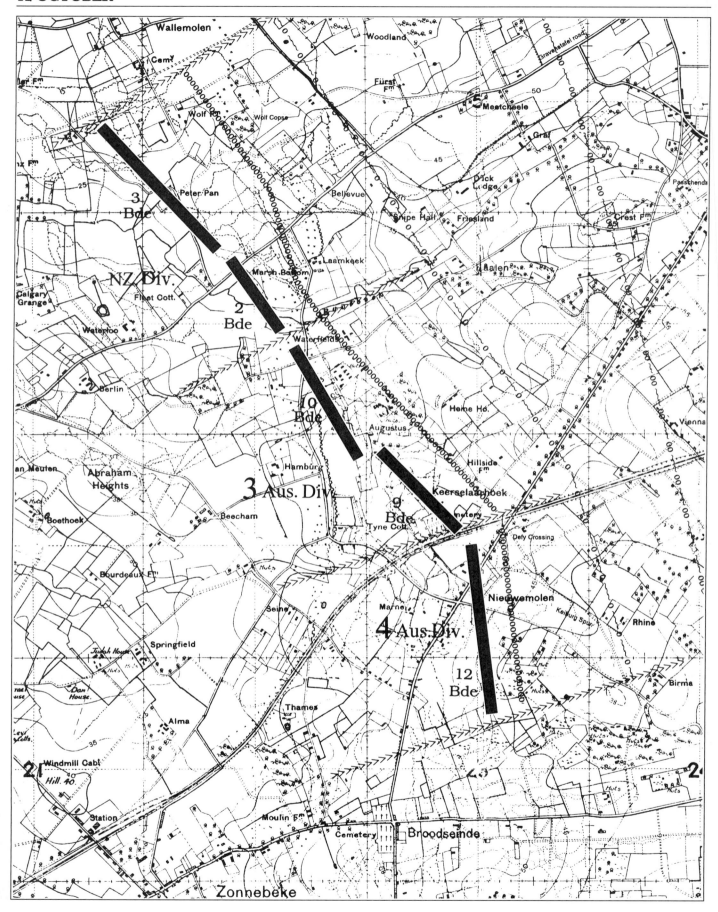

the valley from Bellevue pillboxes. At noon heavy casualties caused the Brigade to begin pulling back to its start line, and by 3.30 p.m. this had been completed.

New Zealand Division

2 NZ Brigade attacked with the 2nd Otago to take the Red Line, the 1st Otago to take the Blue Line and the 1st Canterburys to capture the last objective, the Green Line; the 2nd Canterburys were in reserve.

Attacking at 5.25 a.m., the right struggled up from Marsh Bottom while on the left they were held up by uncut wire around the Gravenstafel road. The 2nd Otago encountered fierce opposition but pushed on to the uncut wire, some 25 to 50 yards deep; this was defended by pillboxes. The only gap in the wire was at a single point on the sunken Gravenstafel road. This proved a death trap to many of the Otagos, who, seeing the rest held up by the wire, rushed the lane, where machine-gun fire mowed them down. The troops on the wire desperately tried to cut paths through and did succeed in getting through the first belt.

The 1st Otago, with survivors from the leading troops, pushed into the gap and tried to crawl under the entanglements, but with little success. The right company in the marshes was held up by two pillboxes, which were taken by hand-to-hand fighting.

The 2nd Canterburys had come up and joined the troops on the high ground but were unable to break through and the men were told to dig in where they were.

3 NZ (Rifle) Brigade formed up with the 2nd Battalion to take the Red Line, the 3rd to take the Blue Line and the 1st to take the Green Dotted Line; the 4th Battalion were in reserve.

Shortly after leaving the start point, part of the 2nd Battalion were held up by an enemy strongpoint. This was cleared. The assaulting troops became intermingled with each other and the 9th Division on their left flank. They captured the Cemetery on their extreme left and established posts 150 yards eastwards. In the centre, parties pushed on to the edge of Wolf Copse, taking Wolf Farm on the way. At 8 a.m. they were ordered to dig in.

A fatigue party clearing mud from a road at St Julien with mud scoops, 12 October. (Q.6057)

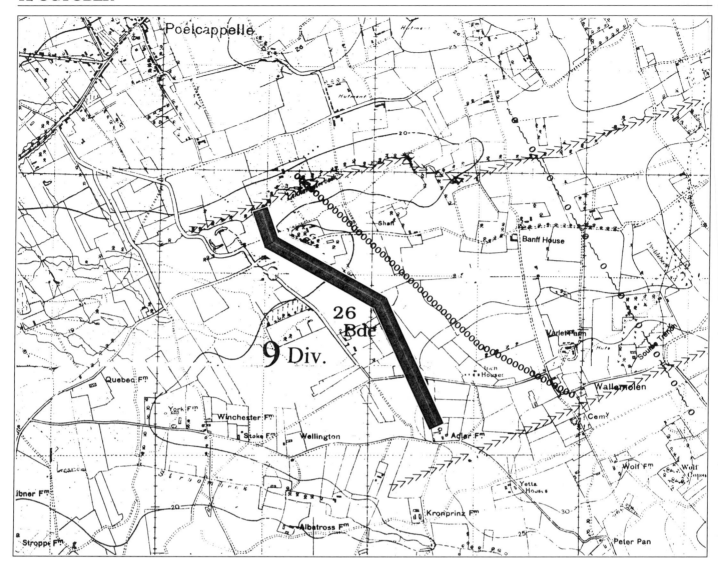

The 1st Battalion, unaware that the attack was held up, came under fire from Peter Pan and Yetta House. They dug in and formed a support line 150 yards west of the road between Wolf Farm and the Cemetery.

At 3 p.m. it was proposed that the attack should be renewed, but this was subsequently cancelled.

XVIII Corps
9th Division
The Division attacked at 5.25 a.m., zero hour, with one brigade.
26 Brigade attacked with the 8th Black Watch and the 10th Argyll & Sutherland Highlanders, with the 7th Seaforths and the 5th Cameron Highlanders in support. The taking of the final objective was allotted to the 6th KOSB, with the 11th and 12th Royal Scots (27 Brigade) in reserve.

The Black Watch took Adler Farm and went on to take the first objective. Parties pushed on and reached Source Trench. The Seaforths advanced through the Black Watch with the Camerons in support, although by this time the Royal Scots had joined the others and a mixed party went on to enter the eastern end of Wallemolen. They were driven out and had to fall back on the Cemetery–Inch House line on the Green Line.

The Argylls lost the barrage almost at once: the troops on the left drifted across the Lekkerboterbeek into the 18th Division area. They advanced 80 yards but were stopped by enemy machine-gun fire from Beek and Meunier Houses. On the right a pill-box held up the whole advance, causing the Royal Scots and the 6th KOSB to back up and become involved in the attack. After this delay they pushed on another 150 yards and consolidated a line of shell holes. The advance had come to a halt 100 yards from their start line.

18th Division
The Division attacked with one brigade, plus one in support.
55 Brigade attacked Poelcapelle and Meunier House at 5.20 a.m. with the 7th West Kents, the 7th Buffs and the 8th East Surreys in single file. The East

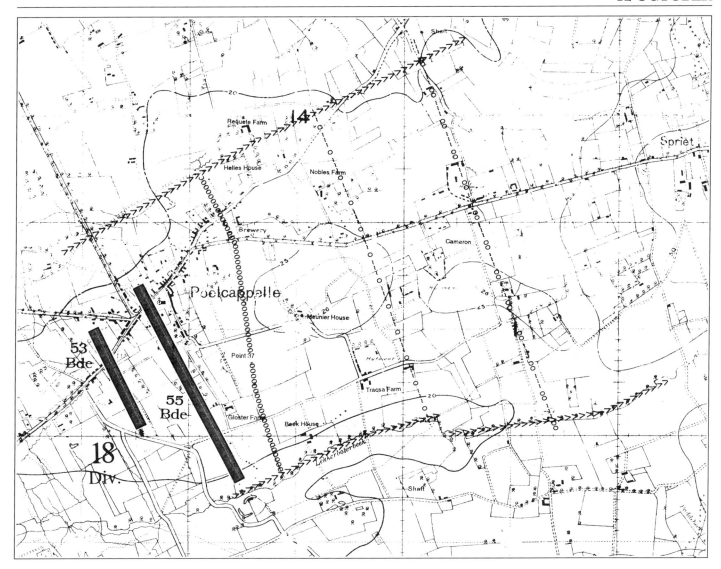

Surreys' advance of at least 500 yards was brought to a halt by fire from two machine guns 100 yards east of Gloster Farm. That evening they were brought back to form a line 100 yards in front of the forming-up tape.

The Buffs attacked with 'D' and 'C' Companies. 'C' Company came under fire almost immediately from Gloster Farm and Point 37; 'D' Company pushed through the houses of Poelcapelle and came under fire from Meunier House and the Brewery, which checked the attack. Posts were dug.

The West Kents, attacking with 'B' Company on the right, made fair progress until coming under fire from the Brewery. They were reinforced by

'D' Company but the fire was too strong and all they could do was establish a series of posts just beyond the original line. 'C' Company pushed on but a strongpoint at the northern end of Poelcapelle brought them to a halt and they dug in.

At noon the Germans launched a counter-attack towards the west of the village; they were beaten off then and on several more occasions during the afternoon.

53 Brigade were in support and had the 8th Suffolks and the 6th Royal Berkshires in the line. A gap between the Suffolks and the 4th Division tempted the Germans twice, once at noon and once at 5.30 p.m.; both attacks were fought off.[69]

XIV Corps
4th Division

The Division attacked at 5.25 a.m., zero hour, with a composite brigade consisting of the 1st Royal Warwickshire Regiment and the Household Battalion; the 1st King's Own (R Lancs[70]) were in support and the 1st Rifle Brigade in reserve.

The Warwicks met little opposition and maintained touch with units on their flanks. The Household Battalion were unable to keep in touch with the left of the 18th Division as they were held up. The advance came under fire from Poelcapelle and in particular from

---

[69]One man in the Suffolks died of exposure that night.
[70]VC: Pte Albert Halton.

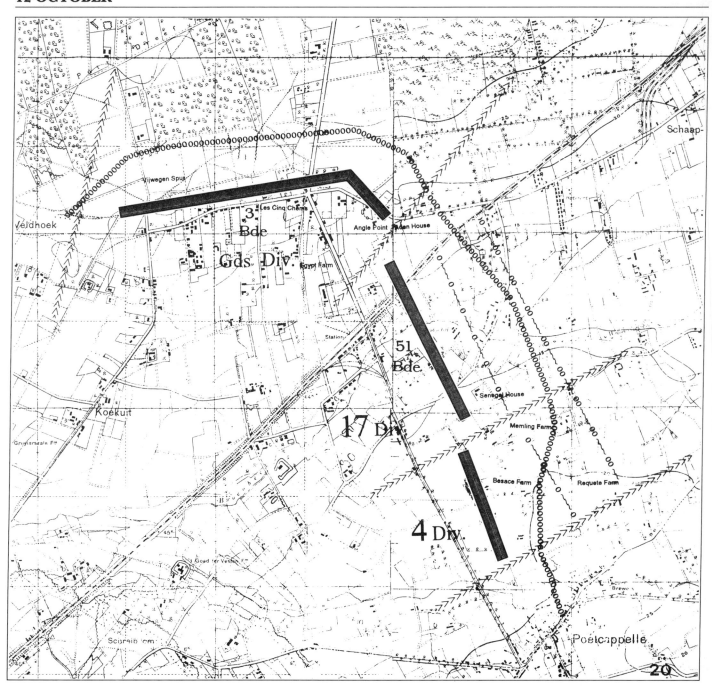

Helles House. A defensive flank was formed with the King's Own, running 500 yards south-west from Requete Farm. At dusk the line was as follows: south-west of Requete Farm–east of Besace Farm–Memling Farm.

17th Division

The Division attacked with one brigade.

51 Brigade attacked at 5.25 a.m. with the 10th Sherwood Foresters on the right and the 7th Lincolns in the centre. The 8th South Staffords, on the left, attacked to the north of the railway. The 7th Border Regiment were in support. The Staffs suffered heavily from machine-gun fire and pulled slightly to the right. In the centre the Lincolns pushed on to the first objective. They missed mopping up a strongpoint in the centre and the garrison of 90 surrendered to three unarmed Lincolns.[71]

By 11 a.m. the second and final objective was taken. The right was at the apex of a sharp salient at Memling Farm and, because the 4th Division was delayed, the Borderers were pushed in to fill the gap.

Guards Division

The Division attacked with one brigade.

3 Guards Brigade: The 4th Grenadier Guards and the 1st Welsh Guards

Left, upper: A pack-horse is loaded at a duckboard dump at Wieltje, 12 October. (Q.6055)

Left, lower: A Holt tractor hauling an 8-inch howitzer at Verbrandenmolen, 13 October. (Q.6071)

Saturday 13 October

Temperature 52°F; 50% cloud cover. Rainfall: 10.7mm.

4th Division (XIV Corps)
The Division was relieved by the 34th Division (XIV Corps).

Sunday 14 October

Temperature 52°F; overcast with showers. Rainfall: nil.

37th Division (IX Corps)
The enemy captured a post on the Division's front.

Monday 15 October

Temperature 52°F; fog, then overcast. Rainfall: nil.

9th Division (XVIII Corps)
South African Brigade: A patrol of the 2nd South African Infantry found Varlet Farm to be occupied by German infantry.

Tuesday 16 October

Temperature 54°F; clear. Rainfall: 0.1mm.

37th Division (IX Corps)
Relieved by the 39th Division (X Corps).

advanced across the western edge of the Vijwegen spur towards the edge of Houthulst Forest during the night of the 11th/12th. The Germans countered this move with a heavy barrage of gas shells.

At 5.25 a.m. the right company of the 4th Grenadiers was brought back to cover the advance of the 1st Grenadiers on their right, who advanced in line with the rest of the Brigade and began to consolidate their position.

The right company of the 4th returned to the positions they had dug the previous night.

Two platoons of the 2nd Scots Guards were sent up to link up with the 17th Division on the right. They did not manage this, but they established themselves in the vicinity of Angle Point. When darkness fell they linked with the 51st Brigade (17th Division) and forced the Germans out of the blockhouses at Angle Point and Aden House.

[71] An orderly in the party summed it up thus: 'The Bosch came out of their pillbox and we had nothing to shoot them with but a basket of blinking pigeons.'

2nd Canadian Division (Canadian Corps)

Relieved by the 48th Division (XVIII Corps).

Wednesday 17 October

Temperature 56°F; clear. Rainfall: 7.1mm.

17th Division (XIV Corps)

Command of the Divisional front was handed over to the 34th, Guards and 35th Divisions (all XIV Corps).

Guards Division (XIV Corps)

Relieved by the 35th Division (XIV Corps).

Thursday 18 October

Temperature 58°F; rain. Rainfall: nil.

3rd Australian Division

9 Australian Brigade were relieved by 148 Brigade, 49th Division (II ANZAC Corps), in the front line. Other brigades were in training.

Friday 19 October

Temperature 48°F; 25% cloud cover. Rainfall: 2.9mm.

Nothing of significance happened on this day.

Saturday 20 October

Temperature 48°F; 75% cloud cover. Rainfall: 2.9mm.

35th Division (XIV Corps)

104 Brigade took up the line Aden House–Les Cinq Chemins.

Sunday 21 October

Temperature 54°F; heavy rain. Rainfall: 1.3mm.

23rd Division (X Corps)
7th Division (XIV Corps)

These two divisions were relieved by the 21st Division (X Corps).

Monday 22 October

Temperature 56°F; overcast. Rainfall: 3.2mm.

3rd Australian Division (II ANZAC Corps)

Relieved by the 4th Canadian Division (Canadian Corps).

18th Division (XVIII Corps)

The Division attacked with one brigade.

53 Brigade attacked at 5.35 a.m. with the 8th Norfolks in the lead, followed by the 10th Essex. A Chinese attack using dummy figures was launched at the same time, to distract the Germans' attention from the imminent attack on the Brewery.

The Norfolks took the Brewery as planned and the Essex, advancing at 7.30 a.m., passed through the Norfolks and went on to take Noble's Farm. They pushed on to Meunier House, which also fell.

After a short barrage, the Essex occupied Tracas Farm, which lay in front of the line. At 5 p.m. about 200 Germans were seen gathering to the rear of Noble's Farm; when they came within range, they were dealt with by Lewis-gun fire.

34th Division (XIV Corps)

The Division attacked at 5.35 a.m. with two brigades.

102 Brigade attacked with the composite battalion 24th/27th Northumberland Fusiliers. They took their objectives and cleared Requete Farm, which had been overlooked by the 18th Division.

101 Brigade attacked with the 15th and 16th Royal Scots. The 15th made their assault on a two-company front, 'A' on the right and 'B' on the left. At 6 a.m. 100 of the enemy advanced towards thirteen men and an officer of 'A' Company and demanded their surrender. They were shot down and only one of the Germans was seen to return to his own lines. 'B' Company reached a point near their objective, a row of pillboxes, which were found still to be occupied by the Germans; they were cut down and only fourteen men returned. The company in support were not able to cross the Broembeek owing to flooding and artillery fire.

The 16th Royal Scots advanced with the 23rd Manchesters on their left (35th Division). They reached their final objective around Six Roads and then put down covering fire for the Manchesters, who tried to outflank the pillboxes but were held up by wire. Later on a strong counter-attack forced them to retire to the east of Egypt House.

The tape line through a shell-hole morass near Alma, north of Zonnebeke, 15 October. (E[AUS].1047)

35th Division (XIV Corps)

The Division attacked with two brigades at 5.35 a.m.

104 Brigade attacked with the 23rd Manchesters and the 17th Lancashire Fusiliers; the 20th Lancashire Fusiliers were in support and the 17th Royal Scots in reserve.

The Manchesters had been unable to gain touch with the 34th Division on their right, but they pushed on and gained their first objective with comparative ease. Resistance stiffened on the way to the next objective, however, and they came under severe machine-gun fire from some huts which had been overlooked in the advance. An isolated party of Manchesters attacked a pillbox near Six Roads, but, by now reduced to fifty men, they pulled back to their original line.

The 17th Lancashire Fusiliers advanced well and passed Colombo House, arriving at the final objective on Conter Drive by 6.45 a.m. A company of 18th Lancashire Fusiliers, in support, wandered too far to the left and entered Houthulst Forest but were forced back to the edge. At 8.35 a.m.

Above: Six-inch shell dumps alongside the road at Birr Crossroads, near Ypres. 1st ANZAC Corps, 17 October. (E[AUS].1991)

Below: A youthful German who lost his life in no man's land during the German attack on 3 October 1917. The photograph was taken near Zonnebeke on 17 October. (E[AUS].927)

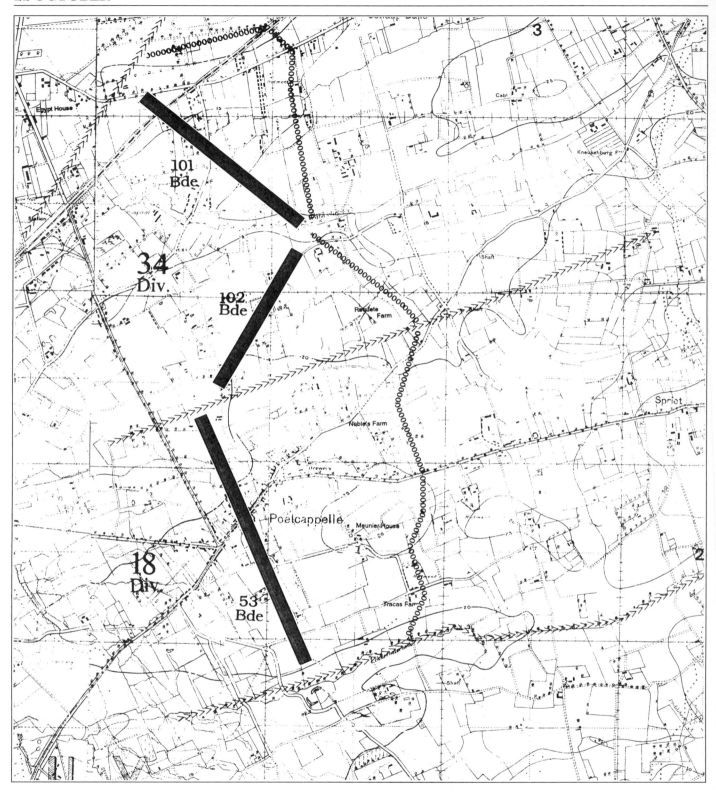

two companies of 20th Lancashire Fusiliers were sent to take up a line which ran from 100 yards in advance of Angle Point to 200 yards in front of Aden House. The position held was consolidated.

105 Brigade attacked with the 16th Cheshires and the 14th Gloucestershires; the 15th Sherwood Foresters were in support and the 15th Cheshires in reserve. The right of the 16th Cheshires went well and gained its

objective, Marechal Farm, with few problems. However, the centre and left were held up by fire from a blockhouse in the wood, 500 yards northwest of Colombo House. The line was consolidated at this point.

On the left, the 14th Gloucesters met strong opposition but occupied their first objective, including Panama House, by 6.15 a.m. Taking two pill-boxes on the way, they reached their final objective and were consolidating by 7.45 a.m. At 4.39 p.m. the Germans launched a counter-attack against the left of the 16th Cheshires and broke through. The surviving Cheshires fell back 100 yards, and then back to their original line. The 14th Gloucesters remained on the original objective and the German attack was caught by artillery fire, but the right of the Gloucesters dropped back and made a defensive flank with the Cheshires. A platoon of the 15th Sherwood Foresters was brought up to bridge the gap.

Tuesday 23 October

Temperature 50°F; showers. Rainfall: 4.0mm.

4th Australian Division (I ANZAC Corps)
Relieved by the 1st Australian Division (I ANZAC Corps).

34th Division (XIV Corps)
Relieved by the 57th Division (XIV Corps).

Wednesday 24 October

Temperature 48°F: 25% cloud cover. Rainfall: 7.7mm.

39th Division (X Corps)
Relieved by the 7th Division (X Corps).

14th Division (II Corps)
Relieved by the 5th Division (X Corps).

35th Division (XIV Corps)
A portion of the Divisional front was taken over by the 50th Division (XIV Corps).

New Zealand Division (II ANZAC Corps)
Relieved by the 3rd Canadian Division (Canadian Corps).

9th Division (XVIII Corps)
Relieved by the 63rd Division (XVIII Corps).

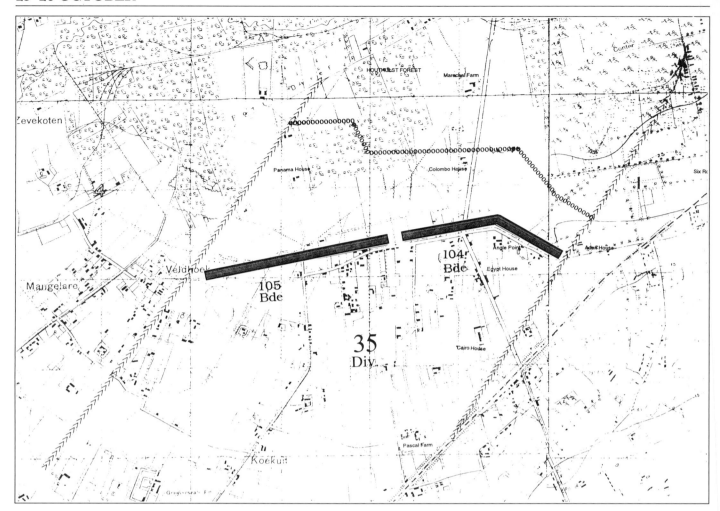

Thursday 25 October

Temperature 50°F; 25% cloud cover. Rainfall: 4.5mm.

18th Division (XVIII Corps)

Relieved by the 58th Division (XVIII Corps).

Friday 26 October

Temperature 48°F; overcast. Rainfall: 7.8mm.

SECOND BATTLE OF PASS-CHENDAELE (26 October–10 November)

SECOND ARMY
X Corps
7th Division

The Division attacked at 5.40 a.m., zero hour, with two brigades.

91 Brigade consisted of the 1st South Staffordshires, the 21st Manchesters and the 2nd Queen's; the 20th Manchesters (from 22 Brigade) were in support.

The Queen's attempted to take Lewis House but were driven back to their start line by machine-gun fire, as were the Manchesters. The Staffs got off to a good start: shielded by the ground from machine-gun fire, they took their first objective, a mound south-west of Hamp Farm. 'D' Company were, however, mown down trying to take Hamp Farm and the same fate befell 'C' Company in their attempt on Berry Cottage.

20 Brigade attacked with the 2nd Border Regiment south of the Menin Road and the 9th Devons, together with the 1st Royal Welsh Fusiliers (22 Brigade) north of the road.

A scene of death and desolation at Garter Point, 24 October. This pillbox commanded a great outlook over the ridges and was captured by the Australians. (E[AUS].1121)

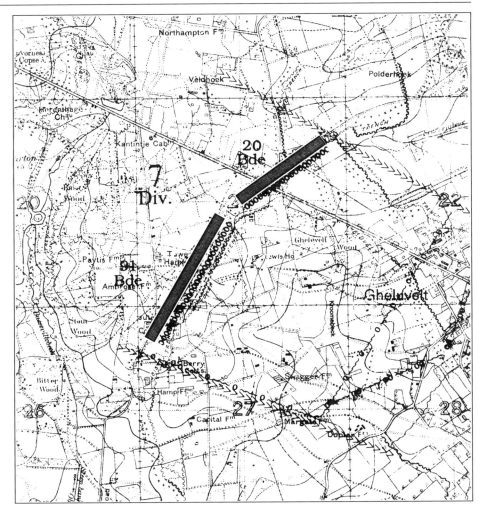

The Border Regiment's right company managed to cross the marsh to the front but as soon as the troops dipped down to the Krommebeck they found themselves waist-deep in the marsh. Machine-gun fire from Swagger Farm behind Berry Cottage accounted for most of the attacking troops. 'D' Company were forced to the left, towards the Menin Road, where they came under fire from pillboxes nearby. Most of the Company became casualties. 'B' Company attacked the pillboxes with no more success. 'A' Company managed to take one of the pillboxes, while the survivors pushed on and got within 100 yards of Gheluvelt Church, establishing themselves about the west end of the village.

The Devons pushed on and managed to establish themselves in a railway cutting north-west of Gheluvelt

Church and others got well into the village. The 8th Devons (in reserve) became mixed up with the 9th, and the mixed group went on with a party clearing some pillboxes on the line of Johnson Trench, almost reaching the church. At 10 a.m. the Germans started counter-attacking and forced all the assaulting troops back out of the village and almost back to their starting line.

5th Division

The Division attacked with one brigade at 5.40 a.m.

13 Brigade attacked with the 1st Royal West Kents, the 15th Royal Warwicks and the 14th Warwicks in line. The West Kents, attacking down the valley of the Scherriabeek, found it an impassable morass. They attempted to push on under fire from Gheluvelt.

125

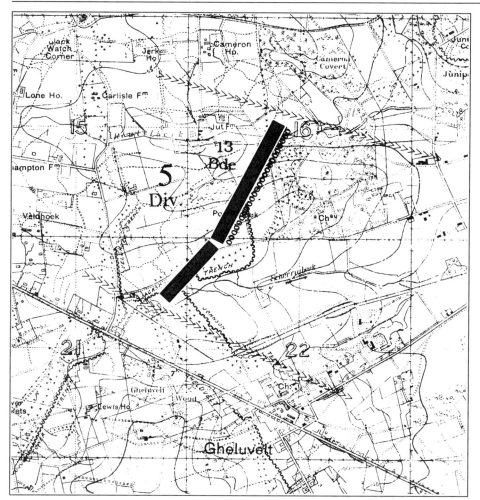

The 15th Warwicks in the centre managed to clear Polderhoek Château and park. On the left the 14th were held up along the Reutelbeek, but the right had got forward enough to link up with the 15th.

The troops in the château pulled back to straighten the line. The Germans reoccupied the strongpoint, machine-gunned the new position and counter-attacked. By evening the attackers had fallen back to their original line.

Canadian Corps
4th Canadian Division
The Division attacked with one brigade.

10 Brigade attacked at 5.40 a.m. with the 46th Battalion astride the Passchendaele road and south of the Ravebeek, and captured the Red Line. Consolidation was carried out under heavy

Hauling up the guns by manpower over ground too soft and wet for horse traffic. Anzac Ridge, 26 October. (E[AUS].1055)

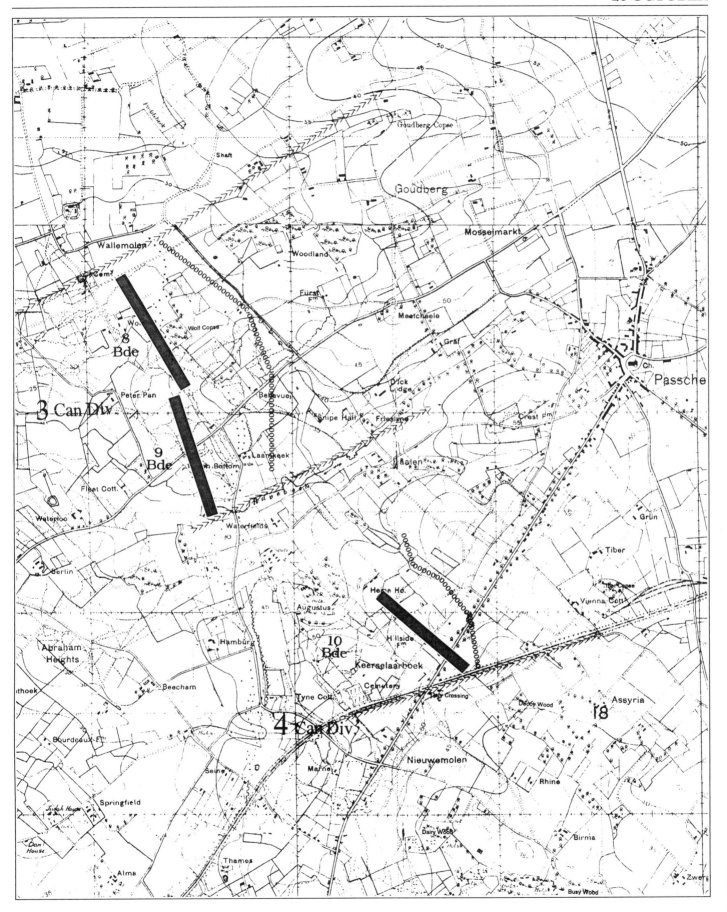

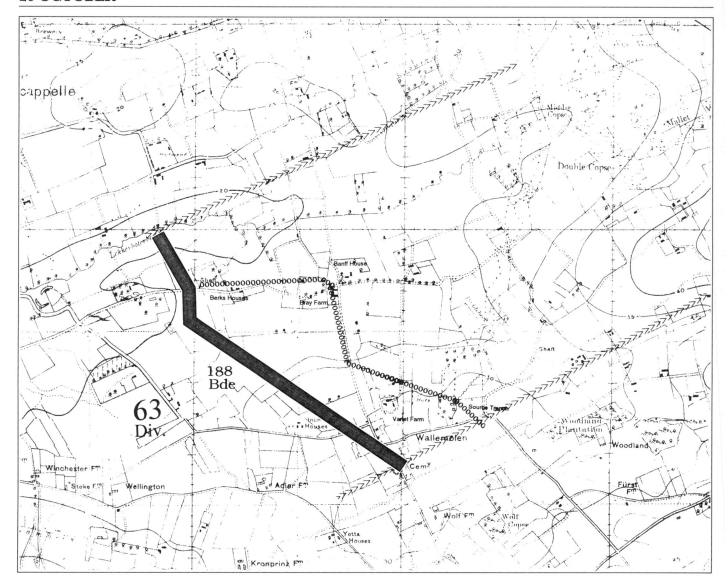

artillery fire from the Germans south-east of Passchendaele.

Of the 420 men of the 46th Battalion who were on the start line at zero hour, 70 per cent became casualties. They were counter-attacked three times during the afternoon and pulled back to within 100 yards of Ravebeek.

3rd Canadian Division

The Division attacked with two brigades at 5.40 a.m.
9 Canadian Brigade attacked with the 43rd[72] and 58th Battalions; the 52nd Battalion[73] were in support. The wire was well cut. The 58th were checked by the Laamkeek strongpoint and the 43rd cleared the Bellevue pillboxes and

went on to the Red Line. But by 9 a.m., under heavy artillery fire, the Brigade was falling back. However, the 43rd managed to keep a foothold on Bellevue.

Around noon the 52nd were sent up. They finished clearing Bellevue and, working south, did the same to Laamkeek. By 6.30 a.m. the next morning the Brigade had consolidated its gains.
8 Canadian Brigade, attacking with the 4th Canadian Mounted Rifles[74], had hard fighting but managed to capture Wolf Copse and secure their part of the objective. They were, however, forced to fall back 300 yards to link up with 63rd Division on their left flank.

FIFTH ARMY
XVIII Corps
63rd Division

The Division attacked with one brigade at 5.40 a.m.
188 Brigade attacked with the Anson Battalion and the 1st Royal Marines; the 2nd Royal Marines were in support and the Howe Battalion in reserve. Two battalions of 189 Brigade were attached, Hood for counter-attacks and Hawke in reserve.

By 7.20 a.m. Anson had captured Varlet Farm; by 8 a.m. Banff House had fallen and the Battalion were consolidating their gains. In the centre, the attack was held up on the road between Bray Farm and Wallemolen. At mid-

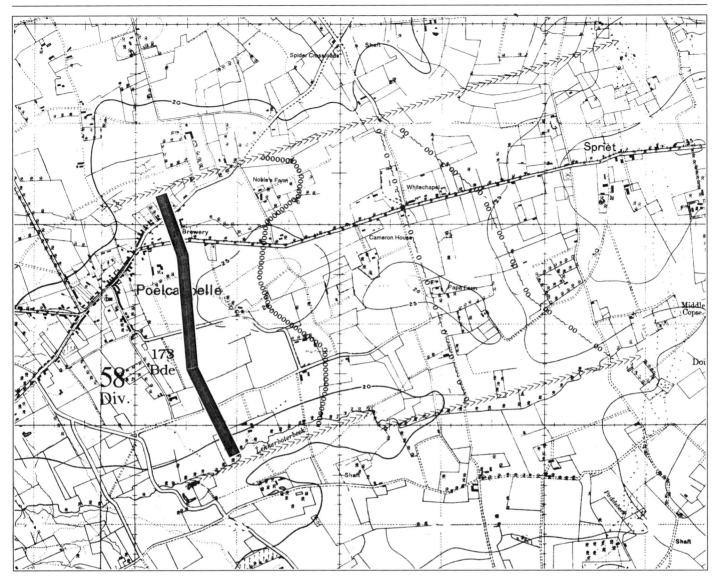

day, Anson were reported to be consolidating around Source Trench.

The 1st Marines had gained their objective on the left but were still held up in the centre just east of the road. The 2nd Marines had intermixed with the first.

Towards nightfall the troops in Banff House were forced to withdraw and now held Berks Houses, and the line turned back westward to the Shaft. The Brigade had gained practically the whole of its first objective except Source Trench and Banff House.

58th Division
The Division attacked at 5.40 a.m., zero hour, with one brigade.

173 Brigade attacked with the 2/2nd and 2/3rd London; the 2/4th London were in support and 2/1st in reserve.

The 2/2nd got off to a good start and captured three of the blockhouses at Cameron House. The 2/3rd advanced to Spider Crossroads, where, totally exhausted and under heavy machine-gun fire, they came to a halt. Between 7 a.m. and 10 a.m. the Germans counter-attacked on the left flank and on Cameron House. With the 57th Division held up, Spider Crossroads was exposed. The Germans forced home their attack, cutting off the advance posts and rolling up the northern gains. At the same time, a strong party of Germans was seen

emerging from the sunken road between Papa Farm and Whitechapel. The 58th were driven back to their original line. The Germans also fell foul of the conditions and were driven off by the 2/4th London, who had been sent up to reinforce.

XIV Corps
57th Division
The Division attacked with one brigade, plus one in reserve.
170 Brigade attacked with the 2/5th, 2/4th and 4/5th Loyal North Lancs; the 2/5th King's Own (R Lancs) were in

[72]VC: Lt Robert Shankland.
[73]VC: A/Capt Christopher Patrick John O'Kelly.
[74]VC: Pte Thomas William Holmes.

129

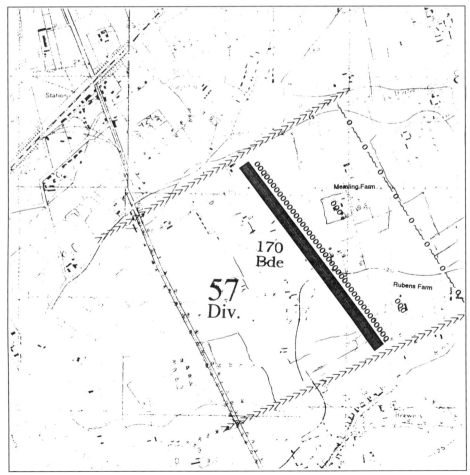

Far left, upper: Canadian Pioneers carrying trench mats. Wounded and prisoners can be seen in the background. (CO.2205)

Far left, lower: Wounded Canadians take cover behind a pillbox. (CO.2211)

Above: Pioneers filling a shell hole. The ambulance was the only material damage; two wounded were inside at the time. (CO.2218)

support, with the 2/8th King's Liverpool Regiment (171 Brigade) in reserve.

The attack was launched at 5.40 a.m. and immediately confronted an impassable morass. The attack came to a stop only a short distance in front of the original line. Two posts were, however, established at Rubens and Memling Farms, about 350 yards and 200 yards, respectively, in advance of the original line.

50th Division
The Division attacked with one brigade at 5.40 a.m.

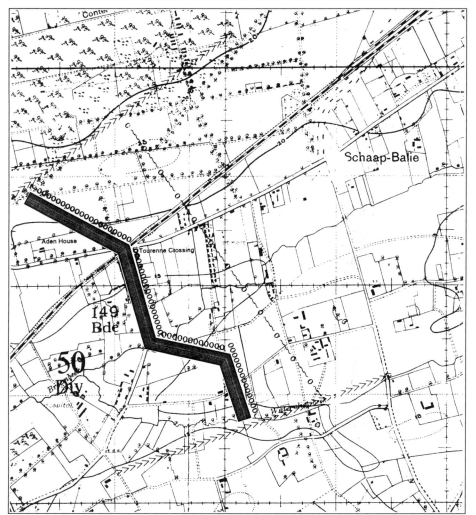

149 Brigade attacked with the 4th, 5th and 7th Northumberland Fusiliers; the 6th were in support. The 4th advanced towards the lines of concrete huts which were its objective. They reached to within 80 yards of them but were stopped by machine-gun fire and sniping. They fell back to their original line and consolidated.

The 5th took their first objective. At 7.40 a.m. troops were seen on Hill 23. They came under machine-gun fire from Houthulst Forest. Fire from the huts was also reported. One platoon of the 6th moved up and occupied the line Aden House–Tourenne Crossing. By 4.15 p.m. the Battalion was back to its original line.

A similar fate befell 7th Battalion. 'A' and 'D' Companies advanced some 2,000 yards, but 'B' Company met with machine-gun fire 100 yards after jump off. They eventually surrounded and passed the concrete huts, but suffered severe casualties.

Owing to very heavy machine-gun fire, the centre and right companies fell back to 150 yards in front of their jumping-off point. The right flank of the left company, being exposed, pulled back in line with the others.

Saturday 27 October

Temperature 49°F; 50% cloud cover. Rainfall: nil.

63rd Division (XVIII Corps)
Hawke Battalion recaptured Banff House. A counter-attack was beaten off with small-arms fire.

4th Canadian Division (Canadian Corps)
The 44th and 47th Battalions were sent up to reinforce, and by 10 a.m. the line of the original objective had been taken.

Sunday 28 October

Temperature 41°F; 50% cloud cover. Rainfall: 1.3mm.

5th Division (X Corps)
Relieved by the 14th Division (X Corps).

5th Australian Division (I ANZAC Corps)
Relieved by the 2nd Australian Division (I ANZAC Corps)

3rd Canadian Division (Canadian Corps)
Patrols were sent out to Meetcheele and Furst Farm.

Monday 29 October

Temperature 47°F; 50% cloud cover. Rainfall: nil.

7th Division (X Corps)
Relieved by 39th Division (X Corps).

1st Australian Division (I ANZAC Corps)
A post was established by the 11th Battalion in Decoy Wood.

Tuesday 30 October

Temperature 44°F; clear, showers. Rainfall: 2.3mm.

Canadian Corps
4th Canadian Division
The Division attacked at 5.50 a.m., zero hour, with one brigade.

12 Canadian Brigade attacked with the 85th, 78th and 72nd Battalions. Although losing half its strength in casualties, the 85th took all the strongpoints in its path, including Vienna Cottage, and consolidated on its target, the Blue Line. The 78th Battalion also took its objective south-east of the Passchendaele road and dug in.

The 72nd captured Crest Farm and then sent patrols into Passchendaele, where they found the Germans evacuating the village. Later the patrols were pulled back to help consolidate the position taken. By 8.30 a.m. the Brigade had taken all its objectives between the railway and the Ravebeek. The left flank was dropped to follow the stream as the 3rd Canadian Division had not kept abreast.

3rd Canadian Division[75]
The Division attacked at 5.50 a.m., zero hour, with two brigades.
7 Canadian Brigade attacked with the Princess Patricia's Canadian Light Infantry[76] and the 49th Battalion[77]. The PPCLI captured Snipe Hall and went on to capture Duck Lodge but came

Men of the 18th Australian Battalion coming from the front lines after the 26 October advance. Near Railway Wood, 28 October. (E[AUS].1073)

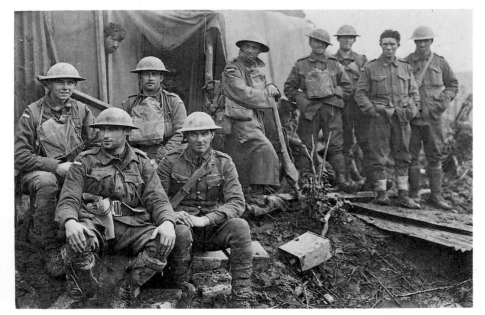

under heavy fire. They took Meetcheele crossroads and dug in. The 49th Battalion, meanwhile, took Furst Farm.
8 Canadian Brigade attacked with the 5th Canadian Mounted Rifles[78]. Although they were held up by the swampy ground of Woodland, they went on to take Source and Vapour Farms. They were reinforced by the 2nd Canadian Mounted Rifles and consolidated.

XVIII Corps
63rd Division
The Division attacked with one brigade at 5.50 a.m., zero hour.
190 Brigade attacked with the Artists Rifles, the 4th Bedfordshires and the 7th Royal Fusiliers; the 1/4th KSLI acted as a counter-attack battalion. The Germans dropped a counter-barrage 100 yards behind the British barrage and caught the attacking troops struggling in the mud; they suffered severe casualties.

The Artists Rifles were holed up near Source Trench. At 7.30 a.m. a message was received that the KSLI thought they had occupied Source Trench but in fact they had occupied the old Canadian front line.

That night the line held by the Division was Source Trench–Varlet Farm–Bray Farm–Berks Houses.

58th Division
The Division attacked with one brigade at 5.50 a.m., zero hour.
174 Brigade attacked with the 2/8th London Regiment and a company of the 2/6th whose task it was to take Noble's Farm and the pillboxes southeast of it.

The 2/8th's barrage was weak and immediately got away from the attacking troops.[79] However, a new line was established 100 yards or so in advance of the original. The 2/6th, on drier ground, found that Noble's Farm had been totally obliterated but succeeded in taking the pillboxes and established a position on a small mound overlooking the Spriet road.

Wednesday 31 October
Temperature 54°F; clear. Rainfall: nil.

50th Division (XIX Corps)
The Division attacked at 2 a.m. on their left flank, with the 1/4th East Yorks and two companies of the 5th Green Howards in support. The centre companies were held up by machine-gun fire, but the flanking companies pushed on to a point only 100 yards short of the objective. The line ran approximately from Turenne Crossing to Colombo House.

63rd Division (XVIII Corps)
189 Brigade were again driven out of Banff House.

1st Australian Division (I ANZAC Corps)
Patrols advanced and found Busy Wood clear of the enemy.

[75] VC: Lt Hugh McKenzie.
[76] VC: Sgt George Harry Mullin.
[77] VC: Pte Cecil John Kinross.
[78] VC: A/Maj George Randolph Pearkes.
[79] The Divisional report states that if the barrage had been as slow as 100 yards in 30 minutes the attacking troops could not have kept up with it.

A line of strafed GS wagons along the
corduroy track accounts for the rations
being late. Bellewaard Ridge, 29
October. (E[AUS].1053)

NOVEMBER

Thursday 1 November

Temperature 51°F; overcast. Rainfall: 0.2 mm.

14th Division (II Corps)

Relieved by the 5th Division (X Corps).

63rd Division (XVIII Corps)

At 8.10 p.m Nelson and Hawke Battalions each captured a German pillbox.

3rd Canadian Division (Canadian Corps)

The enemy assembled at Vapour Farm but did not attack.

4th Canadian Division (Canadian Corps)

A portion of the Divisional line was take over by the 1st Australian Division (I ANZAC Corps).

Canadian wounded are brought through the mud. (CO.2215)

Friday 2 November

Temperature 56°F; overcast. Rainfall: 0.7mm.

3rd Canadian Division (Canadian Corps)

The Germans bombarded the Capitol and Kansas Cross area with gas.

Saturday 3 November

Temperature 52°F; overcast. Rainfall: nil.

63rd Division (XVIII Corps)

Drake Battalion advanced its line to the Paddebeek and attacked and captured Sourd Farm.

3rd Canadian Division (Canadian Corps)

7 Canadian Brigade: At 2 a.m. the 42nd Battalion attacked and took Graf House but were forced out again by machine-gun and rifle fire.

8 Canadian Brigade: At 5.30 a.m. the 1st Canadian Mounted Rifles attacked and captured Vanity and Vine Cottages but were driven out of the latter by a counter-attack.

4th Canadian Division (Canadian Corps)

The enemy attacked in strength from the Ypres–Roulers railway to the Meetcheele–Mosselmarkt road. They gained a foothold at Crest Farm but were driven out by an immediate counter-attack. The Division was relieved by the 2nd Canadian Division (Canadian Corps).

1st Australian Division (I ANZAC Corps)

Troops around Tiber Copse were driven back by the enemy but a coun-

ter-attack re-established their original positions.

Sunday 4 November

Temperature 47°F; overcast. Rainfall: nil.

63rd Division (XVIII Corps)

189 Brigade: Drake Battalion, operating with Hood Battalion, captured some German posts.

3rd Canadian Division (Canadian Corps)

The Division was relieved by the 1st Canadian Division (Canadian Corps).

Monday 5 November

Temperature 49°F; overcast and foggy. Rainfall: nil.

35th Division (XIX Corps)

The Division was relieved by the 18th Division (XIX Corps).

Tuesday 6 November

Temperature 52°F; overcast with showers. Rainfall: 1.0mm.

50th Division (XIX Corps)

The Division's left was relieved by the 18th Division (XIX Corps).

X Corps
5th Division

The Division attacked with one brigade.

95 Brigade attacked with the 1st Devons and the 1st Duke of Cornwall's Light Infantry and immediately came under enemy machine-gun fire from the Polderhoek Château. They reached some shell holes north-west of the château and the Devons, in support of the DCLI, established a line 50 yards to the rear, with their right at a captured pillbox.

The attack broke down into small parties and bombing fights. At 8 a.m. the enemy opened with a very heavy barrage which lasted for two hours. Advance parties were pulled back and then at 3.30 p.m. the left of the line was brought back to its original position. The right was drawn back at dusk and touch was maintained with the Devons in the pillbox.

Canadian Corps
2nd Canadian Division

The Division attacked with one brigade.

6 Canadian Brigade attacked the village of Passchendaele at 6.00 a.m. with the 27th[80], 31st and 28th Battalions. The 27th and 31st met little resistance until they had passed through the village, bayoneting Germans in the ruins and along the main street, when they came under fire from pillboxes on the northern side of the village. The first troops to enter the village were those of the 27th Battalion, and by 8.45 a.m. the entire objective, the village and the eastern crest beyond were firmly in Canadian hands.

The 28th Battalion came under heavy machine-gun fire as it struggled in the mud of Ravebeek valley. However, it managed to catch up with the rest of the Brigade and moved on to its objective.

Visibility being too limited for much air fighting, pilots of both sides amused themselves by strafing each other's infantry. The start line of the 31st received particular attention when German airmen mistook a row of greatcoats for troops.

---

[80]VC: Pte James Peter Robertson.

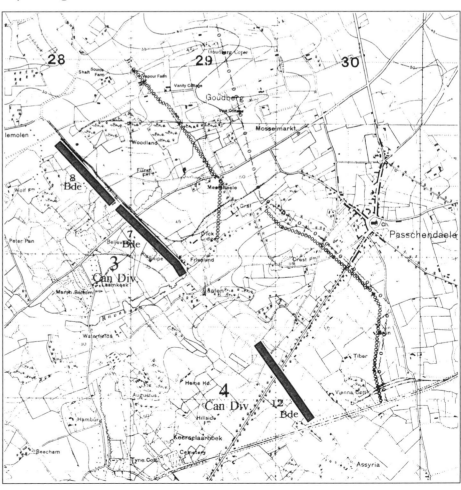

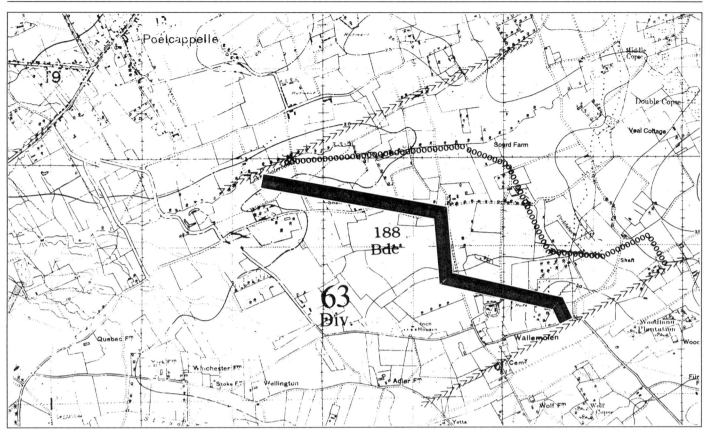

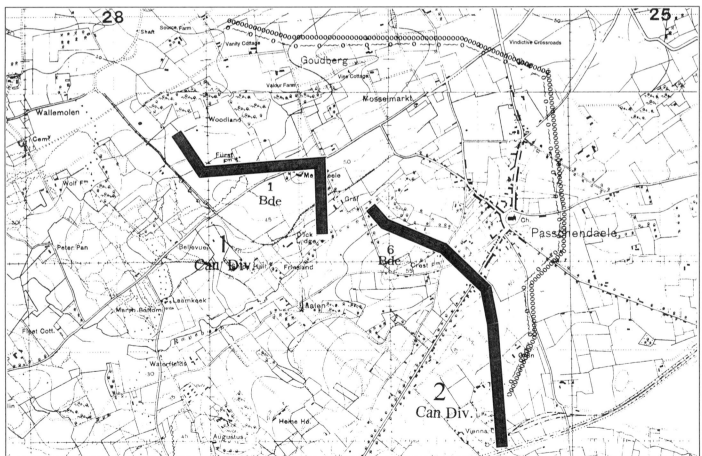

The 5th Canadian Brigade formed a right flank using the 26th Battalion for the purpose.

1st Canadian Division

The Division attacked with one brigade.

1st Canadian Brigade: At 6.00 a.m. the 1st and 2nd Battalions began their assault, which was confined to the Bellevue–Meetcheele spur as the ground to the left was boggy. Little opposition was encountered as they surprised the Germans in the Mosselmarkt blockhouse. By 7.45 a.m. they had taken their objective and consolidation had commenced.

On the other side of the bog the 3rd Battalion[81] met resistance from Vine Cottage but the Germans were driven out and the Battalion went on to its objective.

An enemy counter-attack was threatened but was dealt with by artillery fire.

Wednesday 7 November

Temperature 48°F; overcast. Rainfall: 1.4mm.

Nothing of significance happened on this day.

Thursday 8 November

Temperature 44°F; 25% cloud cover. Rainfall: 2.6mm.

Nothing of significance happened on this day.

Friday 9 November

Temperature 50°F; 50% cloud cover. Rainfall: 1.6mm.

50th Division (XIX Corps)

The remainder of the Division was relieved by the 18th Division (XIX Corps).

Saturday 10 November

Temperature 46°F; rain. Rainfall: 13.4mm.

1st Canadian Division (Canadian Corps)

The Division attacked with two brigades.

4 Canadian Brigade's task was to form a flank with the 20th Battalion, and this it succeeded in doing.

2 Canadian Brigade was to cover the remaining 500 yards to the main ridge east of the Mosselmarkt–Meetcheele road, taking in Venture Farm and Vindictive Crossroads. They attacked at 6.45 a.m. with the 7th and 8th Battalions, supported by the 20th Battalion.

By 7.30 a.m., both units had reached their first objective only 500 yards away. But, in order to hold its position, 7th Battalion on the right had to advance another 300 yards to silence German machine guns in a nearby trench.

The 10th Battalion, moving up from Brigade reserve, took over the whole of the 2nd Canadian Brigade's front, advancing the line to the final objective.

Owing to the failure of the 1st Division, the 8th Battalion was forced to plug the gap and throw back a left flank.

Several counter-attacks were repulsed during the day.

63rd Division (XVIII Corps)

Relieved by the 1st Division (II Corps).

1st Division (II Corps)

The Division attacked with one brigade.

3 Brigade attacked with the 1st South Wales Borderers and the 2nd Munsters. The SWB pulled to the right to avoid the ragged barrage that was falling short in places and a gap developed on the left between them and the Munsters. This prevented Virile Farm and Goudberg Copse from being taken. On the right they did better and established posts near Vocation Farm. They were in touch with the Canadians and dug in.

The first enemy counter-attack was launched at 7.15 a.m. and exploited the gap between the battalions. Holding their position until 1 p.m., the SWB pulled back with their right holding Venture Farm–Valour Farm and then along to Source Farm to link with the Munsters.

The Munsters went well at first, taking their first objective in good time. Void Farm fell after a struggle and was consolidated. Veal and Vat Cottages were all taken easily and by 6.45 a.m. all the Battalion's objectives were achieved.

The Munsters grew tired of awaiting orders and decided to push on to the main ridge 800 yards away. They advanced half way up the ridge and were brought to a stop at 7.30 a.m. while they tried to clean their mud-clogged rifles. At 7.50 a.m. the enemy were spotted massing for a counter-attack. An SOS flare was sent up and the barrage fell on the Munsters, the Artillery having no idea that they had advanced so far.

The attack gradually pushed the Munsters back, but at Void Farm they resisted with the mud equivalent of snowballs and the Germans, thinking these were bombs, fell back. The Germans exploited the weak right flank and 'D' Company was forced back to avoid being cut off. At 8.30 a.m. Void Farm fell to the enemy and, by now, most of the troops were back to their own line and under a savage German bombardment.

At 9.30 a.m. a counter-attack was launched by the Munsters, who managed to take Tournant Farm and consolidate.

The 1st Gloucesters, in support, sent parties to reinforce both the attacking battalions at various times during the day.

[81]VC: Cpl Colin Fraser Barron.

POSTSCRIPT

Third Ypres officially drew to a close on 10 November 1917. The massive artillery bombardments had become a double-edged sword, rendering virtually impassable the ground across which the advance was to be made. Tanks, which should have been a major help to the infantry, floundered in the totally unsuitable conditions. As to the infantry themselves,

. . . the battle will always remain one of the most extraordinary monuments to the courage and endurance of the British soldier. Those hard-used words are indeed inadequate to describe his virtues. If mortal men could have pulled down reinforced concrete with their naked hands, these men would have done it.—Cyril Falls, *History of the Royal Irish Rifles*

APPENDICES

APPENDIX 1
BRITISH AND DOMINION INFANTRY AND PIONEER BATTALIONS, THIRD YPRES, 1917

GUARDS DIVISION
1st Guards Brigade: 2/Gren. Gds; 2/Coldstr. Gds; 3/Coldstr. Gds; 1/Irish Gds
2nd Guards Brigade: 3/Gren. Gds; 1/Coldstr. Gds; 1/Scots Gds; 2/Irish Gds
3rd Guards Brigade: l/Gren. Gds; 4/Gren. Gds; 2/Scots Gds; Welsh Gds
Pioneers: 4/Coldstr. Gds

1st DIVISION
1st Brigade: 10/Gloster; 1/Black Watch; 8/R. Berks; 1/Camerons
2nd Brigade: 2/R. Sussex; 1/L.N. Lancs; 1/Northampton; 2/KRRC
3rd Brigade: 1/SWB; l/Gloster; 2/Welsh; 2/RMF
Pioneers: 1/6th Welsh

3rd DIVISION
8th Brigade: 2/R. Scots; 8/E. Yorks; 1/R. Scots Fus.; 7/KSLI
9th Brigade: l/North'd Fus.; 4/R. Fus.; 13/King's.; 12/W. Yorks
76th Brigade: 8/King's Own; 2/Suffolk; 10/R. Welsh Fus.; 1/Gordons
Pioneers: 20/KRRC

4th DIVISION
10th Brigade: 1/R. Warwick; 2/Seaforth; 1/R. Irish Fus.; 2/R Dub. Fus.
11th Brigade: 1/Somerset L.I.; 1/E. Lancs; 1/Hampshire; 1/Rif. Brig.
12th Brigade: 1/King's Own; 2/Lancs Fus.; 2/Essex; 2/DWR
Pioneers: 21/W. Yorks

5th DIVISION
13th Brigade: 2/KOSB; 1/R. Warwick; 14/R. Warwick; 15/R. Warwick
15th Brigade: 1/Norfolk; 1/Bedford; 1/Cheshire; 16/R. Warwick
95th Brigade: 1/Devon; 1/E. Surrey; 1/DCLI; 12/Gloster
Pioneers: 6/A&SH

7th DIVISION
20th Brigade: 8/Devon; 9/Devon; 2/Border Regt; 2/Gordons
22nd Brigade: 2/R. Warwick; 2/R. Irish; 1/R. Welsh Fus.; 20/Manchester

91st Brigade: 2/Queen's; 1/S. Staffs; 21/Manchester; 22/Manchester
Pioneers: 24/Manchester

8th DIVISION
23rd Brigade: 2/Devon; 2/W. Yorks; 2/Middlesex; 2/Sco. Rif.
24th Brigade: 1/Worcs; 1/Sherwood For.; 2/Northampton; 2/E. Lancs
25th Brigade: 2/Lincoln; 2/R. Berks; 1/R. Irish Rif.; 2/Rif. Brig.
Pioneers: 22/DLI

9th (SCOTTISH) DIVISION
26th Brigade: 8/Black Watch; 7/Seaforth; 5/Camerons; 10/A&SH
27th Brigade: 11/R Scots; 12/R. Scots; 6/KOSB; 9/Sco. Rif.
S. A. Brigade: l/Regt (Cape Prov.); 3/Regt (Trans. & Rhod.); 2/Regt (Natal & OFS) 4/Regt (Scottish)
Pioneers: 9/Seaforth

11th DIVISION
32nd Brigade: 9/W. Yorks; 6/Green Howards; 8/DWR; 6/York & Lanc.
33rd Brigade: 6/Lincoln; 6/Border Regt; 7/S. Staffs; 9/Sherwood For.
34th Brigade: 8/North'd Fus.; 9/Lancs Fus.; 5/Dorset; 11/Manchester
Pioneers: 6/E. Yorks

14th (LIGHT) DIVISION
41st Brigade: 7/KRRC; 8/KRRC; 7/Rif. Brig.; 8/Rif. Brig.
42nd Brigade: 5/O&BLI; 5/KSLI; 9/KRRC; 9/Rif. Brig.
43rd Brigade: 6/Somerset L.I.; 6/DCLI; 6/KOYLI; 10/DLI
Pioneers: 11/King's

15th (SCOTTISH) DIVISION
44th Brigade: 9/Black Watch; 8/Seaforth; 8/10th Gordons; 7/Camerons
45th Brigade: 13/R. Scots; 6/7th R. Scots Fus.; 6/Camerons; 11/A&SH
46th Brigade: 10/Sco. Rif.; 7/8th KOSB; 10/11th HLI; 12/HLI
Pioneers: 9/Gordons

16th (IRISH) DIVISION
47th Brigade: 6/R. Irish; 6/Conn. Rangers; 7/Leinster; 8/RMF
48th Brigade: 7/R. Irish Rif.; 1/RMF; 8/R. Dub. Fus.; 9/R. Dub. Fus.
49th Brigade: 7/R. Innis. Fus.; 8/R. Innis. Fus.; 7/R. Irish Fus.; 8/R. Irish Fus.
Pioneers: 11/Hampshire

17th (NORTHERN) DIVISION
50th Brigade: 10/W. Yorks; 7/E. Yorks; 7/Green Howards; 6/Dorset
51st Brigade: 7/Lincoln; 7/Border Regt; 8/S. Staffs; 10/Sherwood For.
52nd Brigade: 9/North'd Fus.; 10/Lancs Fus.; 9/DWR; 12/Manchester
Pioneers: 7/York & Lanc.

18th (EASTERN) DIVISION
53rd Brigade: 8/Norfolk; 8/Suffolk; 10/Essex; 6/R. Berks
54th Brigade: 11/R. Fus.; 7/Bedford; 6/Northampton; 12/Middlesex
55th Brigade: 7/Queen's; 7/Buffs; 8/E. Surrey; 7/R.W. Kent
Pioneers: 8/R. Sussex

19th (WESTERN) DIVISION
56th Brigade: 7/King's Own; 7/E. Lancs; 7/S. Lancs; 7/L.N. Lancs;
57th Brigade: 10/R. Warwick; 8/Gloster; 10/Worcs; 8/N. Staffs
58th Brigade: 9/Cheshire; 9/R. Welsh Fus.; 9/Welsh; 6/Wiltshire
Pioneers: 5/SWB

20th DIVISION
59th Brigade: 10/KRRC; 11/KRRC; 10/Rif. Brig.; 11/Rif. Brig.
60th Brigade: 6/O&BLI; 6/KSLI; 12/KRRC; 12/Rif. Brig.
61st Brigade: 12/King's; 7/Som L.I.; 7/DCLI; 7/KOYLI
Pioneers: 11/DLI

21st DIVISION
62nd Brigade: 12/North'd Fus.; 13/North'd Fus.; 1/Lincoln; 10/Green Howards
64th Brigade: 1/E. Yorks; 9/KOYLI; 10/KOYLI; 15/DLI
110th Brigade: 6/Leicester; 7/Leicester; 8/Leicester; 9/Leicester
Pioneers: 14/North'd Fus.

23rd DIVISION
68th Brigade: 10/North'd Fus.; 11/North'd Fus.; 12 DLI; 13 DLI
69th Brigade: 11/W. Yorks; 8/Green Howards; 9/Green Howards; 10/DWR
70th Brigade: 11/Sherwood For.; 8/KOYLI; 8/York & Lanc.; 9/York & Lanc.
Pioneers: 9/S. Staffs

24th DIVISION
17th Brigade: 8/Buffs; 1/R. Fus.; 12/R. Fus.; 3/Rif. Brig.
72nd Brigade: 8/Queen's; 9/E. Surrey; 8/R.W. Kent; 1/N. Staffs
73rd Brigade: 9/R. Sussex; 7/Northampton; 13/Middlesex; 2/Leinster
Pioneers: 12/Sherwood For.

25th DIVISION
7th Brigade: 10/Cheshire; 3/Worcs; 8/L.N. Lancs; 1/Wiltshire
4th Brigade: 11/Lancs Fus.; 13/Cheshire; 9/L.N. Lancs; 2/R. Irish. Rif.
75th Brigade: 11/Cheshire; 8/Border Regt; 2/S. Lancs; 8/S. Lancs
Pioneers: 6/SWB

29th DIVISION
86th Brigade: 2/R. Fus.; 1/Lancs Fus.; 16/Middlesex; 1/R. Dub. Fus.
87th Brigade: 2/SWB; 1/KOSB; 1/R. Innis. Fus.; 1/Border Regt
88th Brigade: 4/Worcs; 1/Essex; 2/Hampshire; R. Newfoundand Regt
Pioneers: 2/Monmouth

30th DIVISION
21st Brigade: 18/King's; 2/Green Howards; 2/Wiltshire; 19/Manchester
89th Brigade: 17/King's; 19/King's; 20/King's; 2/Bedford
90th Brigade: 2/R. Scots Fus.; 16/Manchester; 17/Manchester; 18/Manchester
Pioneers: 11/S. Lancs

33rd DIVISION
19th Brigade: 20/R. Fus.; 2/RWF; 1/Sco. Rif.; 5/6/Sco. Rif.
98th Brigade: 4/King's; 4/Suffolk; 1/Middlesex; 2/A&SH
100th Brigade: 1/Queen's; 2/Worcs; 16/KRRC; 1/9 HLI
Pioneers: 18/Middlesex

34th DIVISION
101st Brigade: 15/R. Scots; 16/R. Scots; 10/Lincoln; 11/Suffolk
102nd Brigade: 20/North'd Fus.; 21/North'd Fus.; 22/North'd Fus.; 23/North'd Fus.
103rd Brigade: 24th/27th North'd Fus.; 25/North'd Fus.; 26/North'd Fus.; 9/North'd Fus.
Pioneers: 18/North'd Fus.

35th DIVISION
104th Brigade: 17/Lancs Fus.; 18/Lancs Fus.; 20/Lancs Fus.; 23/Manchester
105th Brigade: 15/Cheshire; 16/Cheshire; 14/Gloster; 15/Sherwood For.
106th Brigade: 17/R. Scots; 17 W. Yorks; 19/ DLI; 18/HLI
Pioneers: 19/North'd Fus.

36th (ULSTER) DIVISION
107th Brigade: 8/R. Irish Rif.; 9/R. Irish Rif.; 10/R. Irish Rif.; 15/R. Irish Rif.
108th Brigade: 11/R. Irish Rif.; 12/R. Irish Rif.; 13/R. Irish Rif.; 9/R. Irish Fus.
109th Brigade: 9/R. Innis. Fus.; 10/R. Innis Fus.; 11/R. Innis. Fus.; 14/R. Irish Rif.
Pioneers: 16/R. Irish Rif.

37th DIVISION
110th Brigade: 8/Leicester; 7/Leicester; 8/Leicester; 9/Leicester
111th Brigade: 10/R. Fus.; 13/R. Fus.; 18/KRRC; 13/Rif. Brig.

112th Brigade: 11/R. Warwick; 6/Bedford; 8/E. Lancs; 10/L.N. Lancs
Pioneers: 9/N. Staffs

38th (WELSH) DIVISION
113th Brigade: 13/R. Welsh Fus.; 14/R. Welsh Fus.; 15/R. Welsh Fus.; 16/R. Welsh Fus.
114th Brigade: 10/Welsh; 13/Welsh; 14/Welsh; 15/Welsh
115th Brigade: 10/SWB; 11/SWB; 17/R. Welsh Fus.; 16/Welsh
Pioneers: 19/Welsh

39th DIVISION
116th Brigade: 11/R. Sussex; 12/R. Sussex; 13/R. Sussex; 14/Hampshire
117th Brigade: 16/Sherwood For.; 17/Sherwood For.; 17/KRRC; 16/Rif. Brig.
118th Brigade: 1/6th Cheshire; 1/1st Cambs; 1/1st Herts; 4/5th Black Watch
Pioneers: 13/Gloster

41st DIVISION
122nd Brigade: 12/E. Surrey; 15/Hampshire; 11/R.W. Kent; 18/KRRC
123rd Brigade: 11/Queen's; 10/R.W. Kent; 23/Middlesex; 20/DLI
124th Brigade: 10/Queen's; 26/R. Fus.; 32/R. Fus.; 21/KRRC
Pioneers: 19/Middlesex

42nd DIVISION
125th Brigade: 5/Lancs Fus.; 6/Lancs Fus.; 7/Lancs Fus.; 8/Lancs Fus.
126th Brigade: 4/E. Lancs; 5/E. Lancs; 9/Manchester; 10/Manchester
127th Brigade: 5/Manchester; 6/Manchester; 7/Manchester; 8/Manchester
Pioneers: None

47th (1/2nd LONDON) DIVISION (TF)
140th Brigade: 1/6th London (City of London); 1/8th London (P.O. Rif.); 1/7th London (City of London); 1/15th London (C.S. Rif.).
141st Brigade: 1/17th London (Poplar & Stepney Rif.); 1/19th London (St Pancras); 1/20th London (Blackheath & Woolwich); 1/18th London (London Irish Rifles)
142nd Brigade: 1/21st London (1st Surrey Rifles); 1/23rd London; 1/22nd London (The Queen's); 1/24th London (The Queen's)
Pioneers: 1/4th R. Welsh Fus.

48th (S. MIDLAND) DIVISION (TF)
143rd Brigade: 1/5th R. Warwick; 1/6th R. Warwick; 1/7th R. Warwick; 1/8th R. Warwick
144th Brigade: 1/4th Gloster; 1/6th Gloster; 1/7th Worcs; 1/8th Worcs
145th Brigade: 1/5th Gloster; 1/4th O&BLI; 1/1st Bucks; 1/4th R. Berks
Pioneers: 1/5th R. Sussex

49th (W. RIDING) DIVISION (TF)
146th Brigade: 1/5th W. Yorks; 1/6th W. Yorks; 1/7th W. Yorks; 1/8th W. Yorks

147th Brigade: 1/4th DWR; 1/5th DWR; 1/6th DWR; 1/7th DWR
148th Brigade: 1/4th KOYLI; 1/5th KOYLI; 1/4th York & Lanc.; 1/5th York & Lanc.
Pioneers: 19/Lancs. Fus.

50th (NORTHUMBRIAN) DIVISION (TF)
149th Brigade: 1/4th North'd Fus.; 1/5th North'd Fus.; 1/6th North'd Fus.; 1/7th North'd Fus.
150th Brigade: 1/4th E. Yorks; 1/4th Green Howards; 1/5th Green Howards; 1/5th DLI
151st Brigade: 1/5th Border Regt; 1/6th DLI; 1/8th DLI; 1/9th DLI
Pioneers: 1/7th DLI

51st (HIGHLAND) DIVISION (TF)
152nd Brigade: 1/5th Seaforth; 1/6th Seaforth; 1/6th Gordons; 1/8th A&SH
153rd Brigade: 1/6th Black Watch; 1/7th Black Watch; 1/5th Gordons; 1/7th Gordons
154th Brigade: 1/9th R. Scots; 1/4th Seaforth; 1/4th Gordons; 1/7th A&SH
Pioneers: 1/8th R. Scots

55th (W. LANCS) DIVISION (TF)
164th Brigade: 1/4th King's; 1/8th King's; 2/5th Lancs Fus.; 1/4th L.N. Lancs
165th Brigade: 1/5th King's; 1/6th King's; 1/7th King's; 1/9th King's
166th Brigade: 1/10th King's Own; 1/10th Kings; 1/5th S. Lancs; 1/5th L.N. Lancs
Pioneers: 1/4th S. Lancs

56th (1/1st LONDON) DIVISION (TF)
167th Brigade: 1/1st London (RF); 1/3rd London (RF); 1/7th Middlesex; 1/8th Middlesex
168th Brigade: 1/4th London (RF); 1/12th London (Rangers); 1/13th London (Kensington); 1/14th London (Lon. Scot.)
169th Brigade: 1/2nd London (RF); 1/5th London (LRB); 1/9th London (QVR); 1/16th London (QWR)
Pioneers: 1/5th Cheshire

57th DIVISION
170th Brigade: 2/5th King's Own; 2/4th L.N. Lancs; 2/5th L.N. Lancs; 4/5th L.N. Lancs
171st Brigade: 2/5th King's; 2/6th King's; 2/7th King's; 2/8th King's
172nd Brigade: 2/9th King's; 2/10th King's; 2/4th S. Lancs; 2/5th S. Lancs
Pioneers: 2/5th L.N. Lancs

58th DIVISION
173rd Brigade: 2/1st London; 2/2nd London; 2/3rd London; 2/4th London
174th Brigade: 2/5th London; 2/6th London; 2/7th London; 2/8th London
175th Brigade: 2/9th London; 2/10th London; 2/11th London; 2/12th London
Pioneers: None

59th DIVISION
176th Brigade: 2/5th S. Staffs; 2/6th S. Staffs; 2/5th N. Staffs; 2/6th N. Staffs
177th Brigade: 2/4th Lincoln; 2/5th Lincoln; 2/4th Leicester; 2/5th Leicester
178th Brigade: 2/5th Sherwood For.; 2/6th Sherwood For.; 2/7th Sherwood For.; 2/8th Sherwood For.
Pioneers:

61st DIVISION
182nd Brigade: 2/5th R. Warwick; 2/6th R. Warwick; 2/7th R. Warwick; 2/8th R. Warwick
183rd Brigade: 2/4th Gloster; 2/6th Gloster; 2/7th Worcs; 2/8th Worcs
184th Brigade: 2/5th Gloster; 2/4th O&BLI; 2/1st Bucks; 2/4th R. Berks
Pioneers: 1/5th DCLI

63rd (RN) DIVISION
188th Brigade: Anson Bn; Howe Bn; 1/R. Marine Bn; 2/R. Marine Bn
189th Brigade: Hood Bn; Nelson Bn; Hawke Bn; Drake Bn
190th Brigade: 1/HAC; 7/R. Fus.; 4/Bedford; 10/R. Dub. Fus.
Pioneers: 14/Worcs

66th DIVISION
197th Brigade: 3/5th Lancs Fus.; 2/6th Lancs Fus.; 2/7th Lancs Fus.; 2/8th Lancs Fus.
198th Brigade: 2/4th E. Lancs; 2/5th E. Lancs; 2/9th Manchester; 2/10th Manchester
199th Brigade: 2/5th Manchester; 2/6th Manchester; 2/7th Manchester; 2/8th Manchester
Pioneers: 10/DCLI

1st AUSTRALIAN DIVISION
1st (NSW) Brigade: 1st Bn; 2nd Bn; 3rd Bn; 4th Bn
2nd (Victoria) Brigade: 5th Bn; 6th Bn; 7th Bn; 8th Bn
9th (Queensland) Brigade: 9th (Q'land) Bn; 10th (S. Austr.) Bn; 11th (W. Austr.) Bn; 12th (S. & W. Austr., Tas.) Bn
Pioneers: 1st Austr. Pioneer Bn

2nd AUSTRALIAN DIVISION
5th (NSW) Brigade: 17th Bn; 18th Bn; 19th Bn; 20th Bn
6th (Victoria) Brigade: 21st Bn; 22nd Bn; 23rd Bn; 24th Bn
7th Brigade: 25th (Q'land) Bn; 26th (Q'land, Tas.) Bn; 27th (S. Austr.) Bn; 28th (W. Austr.) Bn
Pioneers: 2nd Austr. Pioneer Bn.

3rd AUSTRALIAN DIVISION
9th Brigade: 33rd Bn; 34th Bn; 35th Bn; 36th Bn
10th Brigade: 37th Bn; 38th Bn; 39th Bn; 40th Bn
11th Brigade: 41st Bn; 42nd Bn; 43rd Bn; 44th Bn
Pioneers: 3rd Austr. Pioneer Bn

4th AUSTRALIAN DIVISION
4th Brigade: 13th (NSW) Bn; 14th (Vic.) Bn; 15th (Q'land, Tas.) Bn; 16th (S. & W. Austr.) Bn

12th Brigade: 45th (NSW) Bn; 46th (Vic.) Bn; 47th (Q'land, Tas.) Bn; 48th (S. & W. Austr.) Bn
13th Brigade: 49th (Q'land) Bn; 50th (S. Austr.) Bn; 51st (W. Austr.) Bn; 52nd (S. & W. Austr., Tas.) Bn
Pioneers: 4th Aust. Pioneer Bn

5th AUSTRALIAN DIVISION
8th Brigade: 29th (Vic.) Bn; 30th (NSW) Bn; 31st (Q'land, Vic.) Bn; 32nd (S. & W. Austr.) Bn
14th (NSW) Brigade: 53rd Bn; 54th Bn; 55th Bn; 56th Bn
15th (Victoria) Brigade: 57th Bn; 58th Bn; 59th Bn; 60th Bn
Pioneers: 5th Austr. Pioneer Bn

1st CANADIAN DIVISION
1st Brigade: 1st (Ontario) Bn; 2nd (E. Ontario) Bn; 3rd Bn (Toronto Regt); 4th Bn
2nd Brigade: 5th (Western Cav.) Bn; 7th Bn (1st Br. Columbia); 8th Bn (90th Rif.); 10th Bn
3rd Brigade: 13th Bn (R. Highlanders); 14th Bn (R. Montreal Regt); 15th Bn (48th Highlanders); 16th Bn (Canadian Scottish).
Pioneers: 1st Canadian Pioneer Bn

2nd CANADIAN DIVISION
4th Brigade: 18th (W. Ontario) Bn; 19th (Central Ontario) Bn; 20th (Central Ontario) Bn; 21st (E. Ontario) Bn
5th Brigade: 22nd (Canadien Français) Bn; 24th Bn (Victoria Rif.); 25th Bn (Nova Scotia Rif.); 26th (New Brunswick) Bn
6th Brigade: 27th (City of Winnipeg) Bn; 28th (North-West) Bn; 29th (Vancouver) Bn; 31st (Alberta) Bn
Pioneers: 2nd Canadian Pioneer Bn

3rd CANADIAN DIVISION
7th Brigade: PPCLI; R. Cdn. Regt; 42nd Bn (R. Highlanders); 49th (Edmonton) Bn
8th Brigade: 1st Cdn M.R.; 2nd Cdn M.R.; 4th Cdn M.R.; 5th Cdn M.R.
9th Brigade: 43rd Bn (Cameron Highlanders); 52nd (New Ontario) Bn; 58th Bn; 60th Bn (Victoria Rif.)
Pioneers: 3rd Canadian Pioneer Bn

4th CANADIAN DIVISION
10th Brigade: 44th Bn; 46th (S. Saskatchewan) Bn; 47th (Br. Columbia) Bn; 50th (Calgary) Bn
11th Brigade: 54th (Kootenay) Bn; 75th (Mississauga) Bn; 87th Bn (Canadian Grenadier Guards); 102nd Bn
12th Brigade: 38th (Ottawa) Bn; 72nd Bn (Seaforth Highlanders); 73rd Bn (R. Highlanders); 78th Bn (Winnipeg Grenadiers)
Pioneers: 67th Canadian Pioneer Bn

NEW ZEALAND DIVISION
1st NZ Brigade: 1/Auckland; 1/Canterbury; 1/Otago; 1/Wellington
2nd NZ Brigade: 2/Auckland; 2/Canterbury; 2/Otago; 2/Wellington
3rd NZ (Rifle) Brigade: 1/NZRB; 2/NZRB; 3/NZRB; 4/NZRB
Pioneers: NZ Pioneer Bn

APPENDIX 2
GERMAN ORDER OF BATTLE, THIRD YPRES, 1917

BAVARIAN ERSATZ DIVISION
4 and 15 Bavarian Reserve Regts; 28 Ersatz Regt

1st BAVARIAN RESERVE DIVISION
1, 2 and 3 Bavarian Reserve Regts

2nd GUARD RESERVE DIVISION
71, 82 and 94 Reserve Regts

3rd GUARD DIVISION
Gd Fus. and Lehr Regts; 9 Gren. Regt

3rd RESERVE DIVISION
2 and 49 Reserve Regts; 34 Fus. Regt

3rd NAVAL DIVISION
1, 2 and 3 Marine Regts

4th GUARD DIVISION
5 Ft Regt; 5 Gren. Regt; 93 Reserve Regt

4th DIVISION
14, 49 and 140 Regts

4th BAVARIAN DIVISION
5 Bavarian, 5 Bavarian Reserve and 9 Bavarian Regts

5th BAVARIAN DIVISION
1, 19 and 21 Bavarian Regts

5th BAVARIAN RESERVE DIVISION
10, 7 and 12 Bavarian Reserve Regts

6th BAVARIAN DIVISION
10, 6 and 13 Bavarian Regts

6th BAVARIAN RESERVE DIVISION
16, 17 and 20 Bavarian Reserve Regts

7th DIVISION
26, 163 and 393 Regts

8th DIVISION
72, 93 and 153 Regts

8th BAVARIAN RESERVE DIVISION
18,19, 22 and 23 Bavarian Reserve Regts

9th RESERVE DIVISION
6 and 19 Reserve Regts; 395 Regt

9th BAVARIAN RESERVE DIVISION
11 and14 Bavarian Reserve Regt; 3 Bavarian Ersatz Regt

10th ERSATZ DIVISION
369, 370 and 371 Regts

10th BAVARIAN DIVISION
16 Bavarian Regt; 6 Regt; 8 Bavarian Reserve Regt

11th RESERVE DIVISION
10 Reserve Regt; 22 and 156 Regts

11th BAVARIAN DIVISION
13 Bavarian Reserve Regt; 3 and 22 Regts

12th DIVISION
23, 62 and 63 Regts

12th RESERVE DIVISION
22, 38 and 51 Reserve Regts

15th DIVISION
69, 160 and 389 Regts

15th BAVARIAN DIVISION
30, 31 and 32 Bavarian Regts

16th DIVISION
28, 29 and 68 Regts

16th BAVARIAN DIVISION
8, 11 and 14 Bavarian Regts

17th DIVISION
75 Regt; 89 Gren. Regt; 90 Fus. Regt

17th RESERVE DIVISION
16 and 162 Regts; 78 Reserve Regt

18th DIVISION
31 and 85 Regts; 86 Fus. Regt

18th RESERVE DIVISION
31, 84 and 86 Regts

19th RESERVE DIVISION
73, 78 and 92 Reserve Regts

20th DIVISION
77, 79 and 92 Regts

22nd DIVISION
82, 83 and 167 Regts

22nd RESERVE DIVISION
71, 82 and 94 Reserve Regts

23rd RESERVE DIVISION
100 Reserve Gren. Regt; 102 Reserve Regt; 392 Regt

24th DIVISION
133, 139 and 179 Regts

25th DIVISION
115 Body Gd. Inf. Regt; 116 and 117 Body Inf. Regts

25th RESERVE DIVISION
83 and 118 Reserve Regts; 168 Regt

26th DIVISION
119 Gren. Regt; 121 and 125 Regts

26th RESERVE DIVISION
119 and 121 Reserve Regts; 180 Regt

27th DIVISION
123 Gren. Regt; 120 and 124 Regts

32nd DIVISION
102, 177 and 103 Regts

34th DIVISION
67, 30 and 145 Regts

35th DIVISION
141, 61 and 176 Regts

36th DIVISION
5 Gren. Regt; 175 and 128 Regts

38th DIVISION
94, 95 and 96 Regts

39th DIVISION
126, 132 and 172 Regts

40th DIVISION
104, 181 and 134 Regts

41st DIVISION
18, 148 and 152 Regts

44th RESERVE DIVISION
205, 206 and 208 Reserve Regts

45th RESERVE DIVISION
210, 211 and 212 Reserve Regts

49th RESERVE DIVISION
225, 226 and 228 Reserve Regts

50th RESERVE DIVISION
229, 230 and 231 Reserve Regts

52nd RESERVE DIVISION
238, 239 and 240 Reserve Regts

54th DIVISION
84 and 27 Reserve Regts; 90 Reserve Regt

54th RESERVE DIVISION
246, 247 and 248 Reserve Regts

58th DIVISION
106 and 107 Regts; 103 Reserve Regt

79th RESERVE DIVISION
261, 262 and 263 Reserve Regts

111th DIVISION
73 Fus. Regt; 76 and 164 Regts

119th DIVISION
46, 58 and 46 Reserve Regts

121st DIVISION
60 Regt; 7 and 56 Reserve Regts

183rd DIVISION
184, 418 and 440 Reserve Regts

185th DIVISION
65, 161 and 28 Regts

187th DIVISION
187, 188 and 189 Regts

195th DIVISION
6 and 8 Jäg. Regts; 233 Reserve Regt

199th DIVISION
114 and 357 Regts; 237 Reserve Regt

204th DIVISION
413 and 414 Regts; 120 Reserve Regt

207th DIVISION
98, 209 and 213 Reserve Regts

208th DIVISION
25 and 185 Regts; 65 Reserve Regt

214th DIVISION
50, 358 and 363 Regts

220th DIVISION
190 Regt; 55 and 99 Reserve Regts

221st DIVISION
41 and 60 Reserve Regts; 1 Reserve Ersatz Regt

227th DIVISION
417, 441 and 477 Regts

231st DIVISION
442, 443 and 444 Regts

233rd DIVISION
448, 449 and 450 Regts

234th DIVISION
451, 452 and 453 Regts

235th DIVISION
454, 455 and 456 Regts

236th DIVISION
457, 458 and 459 Regts

238th DIVISION
463, 464 and 465 Regts

239th DIVISION
466, 467 and 468 Regts

240th DIVISION
469, 470 and 471 Regts

APPENDIX 3
VICTORIA CROSSES AWARDED DURING THIRD YPRES

An asterisk (*) after a name indicates a posthumous award; the symbol § denotes a bar to the VC.

Date	Name	Rank/unit	Place of deed
31 July 1917	Andrew, Leslie Wilton	Cpl (later Brig), 2 Bn Wellington Inf. Regt, NZ Div., NEF	La Basse-Ville, Belgium
	Bye, Robert James	Sgt, 1 Bn Welsh Guards, Guards Div., BEF	Yser Canal, Belgium
	Chavasse, Noel Godfrey*§	Capt RAMC (Att. 1/10th King's Liverpool Regt), 55 Div., BEF	Wieltje, Belgium
	Coffin, Clifford	T/Brig-Gen (later Maj-Gen), Corps of Royal Engineers, Cdr 25 Inf. Bde, 8 Div., BEF	Westhoek, Belgium
	Colyer-Fergusson, Thomas Riverdale*	A/Capt, 2 Bn Northamptonshire Regt, 8 Div., BEF	Bellewaarde, Belgium
	Davies, James Llewellyn*	Cpl, 13 Bn Royal Welsh Fus., 38 Div., BEF	Polygon Wood, Pilckem, Belgium
	Dunkley, Bertram Best*	T/Lt-Col, Cdr 2/5 Bn, Lancashire Fus., 55 Div., BEF	Wieltje, Belgium
	Edwards, Alexander	Sgt, 1/6th Bn Seaforth Highlanders, 51 Div., BEF	N of Ypres, Belgium
	Hewitt, Dennis George Wyldbore*	2/Lt, 14 Bn Hampshire Regt, 39 Div., BEF	NE of Ypres, Belgium
	Mayson, Tom Fletcher	L-Sgt, 1/4 Bn King's Own (Royal Lancaster) Regt, 55 Div., BEF	Wieltje, Belgium
	McIntosh, George Imlach	Pte (later Flt Sgt), 1/6 Bn Gordon Highlanders, 51 Div., BEF	Ypres, Belgium

	Rees, Ivor	Sgt (later Coy Sgt-Maj), 11th Bn South Wales Borderers, 38 Div., BEF	Pilckem, Belgium
	Whitham, Thomas	Pte, 1 Bn Coldstream Guards, Guards Div., BEF	Pilckem, Belgium
1 Aug. 1917	Ackroyd, Harold*	T/Capt, RAMC, att. 6 Bn Royal Berkshire Regt (Princess Charlotte of Wales's), 18 Div., BEF	Ypres, Belgium
11 Aug. 1917	Loosemore, Arnold	Pte (later Sgt), 8 Bn Duke of Wellington's (West Riding) Regt, 11 Div., BEF	S of Langemarck, Belgium
16 Aug. 1917	Cooper, Edward	Sgt (later Maj), 12 Bn King's Royal Rifle Corps, 20 Div., BEF	Langemarck, Belgium
	Edwards, Wilfred	Pte (later Capt), 7 Bn King's Own Yorkshire Light Inf., 20 Div., BEF	Langemarck, Belgium
	Grimbaldeston, William Henry	A/Coy QMS,1 Bn King's Own Scottish Borderers, 29 Div., BEF	Wijdendrift, Belgium
	Room, Frederick George	A/L-Cpl, 2nd Bn Royal Irish Regt, 16 Div., BEF	Frezenburg, Belgium
18 Aug. 1917	Skinner, John	A/Coy Sgt-Maj, 1 Bn King's Own Scottish Borderers, 29 Div., BEF	Wijdendrift, Belgium
8 Sept. 1917	Carmichael, John	Sgt, 9 Bn North Staffordshire Regt (Prince of Wales's), 37 Div., BEF	Hill 60, Zwarteleen, Belgium
13 Sept. 1917	Moyney, John	L-Sgt (later Sgt), 2 Bn Irish Guards, Guards Div., BEF	Broembeek, Belgium
	Woodcock, Thomas	Pte (later Cpl), 2 Bn Irish Guards, Guards Div., BEF	N of Broembeek, Belgium
20 Sept. 1917	Birks, Frederick*	2/Lt, 6 (Victoria) Bn, 1 Austr. Div., AIF	Glencorse Wood, E of Ypres, Belgium
	Burman, William Francis	Sgt, 16 Bn Rifle Bde (Prince Consort's Own), 39th Div., BEF	SE of Ypres, Belgium
	Colvin, Hugh	2/Lt (later Maj), 9 Bn Cheshire Regt, 19th Div., BEF	E of Ypres, Belgium
	Egerton, Ernest Albert	Cpl (later Sgt),16 Bn Sherwood Foresters (Notts & Derbys Regt), 39 Div., BEF	SE of Ypres, Belgium
	Hewitt, William Henry	L-Cpl (later Maj), 2 Bn South African Light Inf., 9 Div., BEF	E of Ypres, Belgium
	Inwood, Reginald Roy	Pte (later Sgt), 10 (S. Austr.) Bn, 1st Austr. Div., AIF	Polygon Wood, nr Ypres, Belgium
	Knight, Alfred Joseph	Sgt (later 2/Lt), 2/8 Bn (City of London), 58 Div., BEF	Alberta Section, Ypres, Belgium
	Moore, Montague Shadworth Seymour	2/Lt (later Maj), 15t Bn, Hampshire Regt, 41 Div., BEF	Nr Tower Hamlets, E of Ypres, Belgium
	Reynolds, Henry	T/Capt, 12 Bn Royal Scots (Lothian Regt), 9 Div., BEF	Frezenburg, Belgium
26 Sept. 1917	Budgen, Patrick Joseph*	Pte, 31 Bn (Q&V), 5 Austr. Div., AIF	Polygon Wood, nr Ypres, Belgium
	Dwyer, John James (later The Hon.)	Sgt (later Lt), 4 Coy Machine Gun Corps, AIF	Zonnebeke, Belgium
	Hamilton, John Brown	A/L-Cpl (later Sgt), 1/9 Bn Highland Light Inf., 33 Div., BEF	N of Ypres–Menin Road, Belgium
1 Oct. 1917	Bent, Philip Eric*	T/Lt-Col, Cdr 9 Bn Leicestershire Regt, 21st Div., BEF	Polygon Wood, nr Ypres, Belgium
4 Oct. 1917	Coverdale, Charles Harry	Sgt (later 2/Lt), 11 Bn Manchester Regt, 11 Div., BEF	Poelcapelle, Belgium

149

APPENDICES

	Evans, Lewis Pugh	A/Lt-Col (later Brig-Gen), Black Watch Regt, Cdr 1 Bn Lincolnshire Regt, 21 Div., BEF	Nr Zonnebeke, Belgium
	Greaves, Fred	A/Cpl (later Sgt), 9 Bn Sherwood Foresters (Notts & Derbys Regt), 11 Div., BEF	Poelcapelle, Belgium
	Hutt, Arthur	Pte (later Cpl), 1/7 Bn Royal Warwickshire Regt, 48 Div., BEF	Terrier Farm, SE of Poelcapelle, Belgium
	McGee, Lewis*	Sgt, 40 (Tasmania) Bn, 3 Austr. Div., AIF	E of Ypres, Belgium
	Ockenden, James	Sgt, 1 Bn Royal Dublin Fus., 29 Div., BEF	E of Langemarck, Belgium
	Peeler, Walter	L-Cpl (later Sgt), 3 Pioneer Bn, 3 Austr. Div., AIF	E of Ypres, Belgium
	Robertson, Clement*	A/Capt, Queen's Royal West Surrey Regt (att. Special Reserve, Tank Corps), BEF (in support of 21 Div.)	Zonnebeke, Belgium
	Sage, Thomas Henry	Pte, 8 Bn Somerset Light Inf. (Prince Albert's), 37 Div., BEF	Tower Hamlets Spur, E of Ypres, Belgium
9 Oct. 1917	Clamp, William*	Cpl, 6 Bn Yorkshire Regt, 11 Div., BEF	Poelcapelle, Belgium
	Dancox, Frederick George	Pte, 4 Bn Worcestershire Regt, 29 Div., BEF	Boesinghe Sector, Belgium
	Lister, Joseph	Sgt, 1 Bn Lancashire Fus., 29 Div., BEF	E of Ypres, Belgium
	Molyneaux, John	Sgt, 2 Bn Royal Fus., 29th Div., BEF	Langemarck, Belgium
	Rhodes, John Harold	L-Sgt, 3 Grenadier Guards, Guards Div., BEF	Nr Houthulst Forest, E of Ypres,
12 Oct. 1917	Halton, Albert	Pte, 1 Bn King's Own (Royal Lancaster) Regt, 4th Div., BEF	Nr Poelcapelle, Belgium
	Jeffries, Clarence Smith*	Capt, 34 (NSW) Bn, 3 Austr. Div., AIF	Passchendaele, Belgium
26 Oct. 1917	Holmes, Thomas William	Pte, 4 Bn Canadian Mounted Rifles, 3 Can. Div., CEF	Nr Passchendaele, Belgium
	O'Kelly, Christopher Patrick John	A/Capt (later Maj), 52 Manitoba Regt, 3 Can. Div., CEF	Passchendaele, Belgium
	Shankland, Robert	Lt (later Lt-Col), 43 Manitoba Regt, 3 Can. Div., CEF	Passchendaele, Belgium
30 Oct. 1917	Kinross, Cecil John	Pte, 49 Bn Alberta Regt, 3 Can. Div., CEF	Passchendaele, Belgium
	McKenzie, Hugh*	Lt, 7 Coy Canadian Machine Gun Corps, 3 Can. Div., CEF	Meetscheele Spur, nr Passchendaele, Belgium
	Mullin, George Harry	Sgt (later Maj), Princess Patricia's Canadian Light Inf., 3 Can. Div., CEF	Passchendaele, Belgium
	Pearkes, George Randolph (later The Hon.)	A/Maj (later Maj-Gen), 5 Bn Canadian Mounted Rifles, 3 Can. Div., CEF	Nr Passchendaele, Belgium
6 Nov. 1917	Barron, Colin Fraser	Cpl (later Sgt), 3 Bn (Toronto Regt), 1 Can. Div., CEF	Passchendaele, Belgium
	Robertson, James Peter*	Pte, 27 Manitoba Bn, 2 Can. Div., CEF	Passchendaele, Belgium

SELECT BIBLIOGRAPHY AND SOURCES

Anon., *The 54th Infantry Brigade, 1914–1918*, Gale and Polden, 1919

Anon., 'The Register of the Victoria Cross', *This England*, 1988

Anon., *Sixteenth; Seventeenth; Eighteenth; Nineteenth Battalions: The Manchester Regiment, a Record*, Manchester, 1923

Anon. (Committee), *History of the East Lancashire Regiment in the Great War 1914–1918*, Littlebury Brothers, 1936

Anon. (Regimental History Committee), *History of the Dorsetshire Regiment,1914–1919*, Henry Ling, 1932

Atkinson, C. T., *The Devonshire Regiment 1914–1918*, Eland Brothers and Simpkin, Marshall, Hamilton, Kent & Co., 1926

———, *The History of the South Wales Borderers,1914–1918*, Medici Society, 1931

———, *The Queen's Own Royal West Kent Regiment 1914–1919*, Simpkin, Marshall, Hamilton, Kent & Co., 1924

———, *The Seventh Division*, John Murray, 1927

Atteridge, A. Hilliard, *History of the 17th (Northern) Division*, Robert Maclehose & Co., 1929

Bean, C. E. W., *The Official History of Australia in the War of 1914–1918*, University of Queensland Press (in association with Australian War Memorial), 1933

Bewsher, Maj F. W., *The History of the 51st (Highland) Division 1914–1918*, William Blackwood & Sons, 1921

Bond, Lt-Col Reginald C., *History of the King's Own Yorkshire Light Infantry in the Great War 1914–1918*, Percy, Lund Humphries & Co., 1929

Boraston Lt-Col J. H., and Bax, Capt Cyril E. O., *The Eighth Division in War, 1914–1918*, Medici Society, 1926

Coop, Rev. J. O., 'The Story of the 55th (West Lancashire) Division', *Liverpool Daily Post*, 1919

Denman, Terence, *Ireland's Unknown Soldiers*, Irish Academic Press, 1992

Dudley Ward, Maj C. H., *The 56th Division*, John Murray, 1921

———, *Regimental Records of the Royal Welch Fusiliers (23rd Foot)*, Forster Groom & Co Ltd, 1928

Edmonds, Brig-Gen Sir James E., *Military Operations France and Belgium, 1917*, HMSO, 1948

Ewing, John, M. C., *The History of the 9th (Scottish) Division 1914–1919*, John Murray, 1921

Falls, Cyril, *The History of the 36th (Ulster) Division*, Somme Association, 1922/1992

———, *The History of the First Seven Battalions: The Royal Irish Rifles*, Gale and Polden, 1925

Gibbon, Frederick P., 'The 42nd (East Lancashire Division 1914–1918', *Country Life*, 1920

Grimwade, Capt. F. Clive, *The War History of the 4th Battalion The London Regiment (Royal Fusiliers)*, HQ of 4th London Regiment, 1922

Headlam, Cuthbert, *History of the Guards Division in the Great War 1915–1918*, John Murray, 1924

Inglefield, Capt V. E., *The History of the Twentieth (Light) Division*, Nesbit & Co., 1921

James, Brig E. A., *Historical Records of British Infantry Regiments in the Great War 1914–1918*, privately printed by Rank Xerox, 1976

Jerrold, Douglas, *The Royal Naval Division*, Hutchinson & Co., 1923

Keeson, Maj C. A. Cuthbert, *The History and Records of Queen Victoria's Rifles 1792–1922*, Constable & Co., 1923

Kincaid-Smith, Lt-Col M., *The 25th Division in France and Flanders*, Harrison & Sons, 1918

Latter, Maj-Gen J. C., *The History of the Lancashire Fusiliers 1914–1918*, Vols I and II, Gale and Polden, 1949

Maude, Alan H., *The History of the 47th (London) Division 1914–1919*, Amalgamated Press, 1922

Mockler-Ferryman, Lt-Col A. F., *The Oxfordshire and Buckinghamshire Light Infantry Chronicle, 1917–1918*, Eyre & Spottiswoode, ?1920

Moody, Col. R. S. H., *Historical Records of The Buffs, 1914–1919*, Medici Society, 1922

Munby, Lt-Col J. E., *A History of the 38th (Welsh) Division*, Hugh Rees, 1920

Nichols, Capt G. H. F. (Quex), *The 18th Division in the Great War*, William Blackwood & Sons, 1922

Nicholson, Col G. W. L., *Official History of the Canadian Army in the First World War*, Roger Duhamel (with permission Dept of National Defence), 1962

O'Neill, H.C., *The Royal Fusiliers in the Great War*, William Heinemann, 1922

Pearse, Col H. W., and Sloman, Brig-Gen H. S., *History of the East Surrey Regiment. Vol. III: 1917–1919*, Medici Society, 1924

SELECT BIBLIOGRAPHY

Sandilands, Lt-Col H. R., *The 23rd Division 1914–1919*, William Blackwood & Sons, 1925

Seton Hutchison, Lt-Col Graham, *The Thirty-Third Division in France and Flanders 1915–1919*, Waterlow & Sons, 1921

Seymour, William W., *The History of The Rifle Brigade in the War of 1914–1918*, Vol. II, The Rifle Brigade Club, 1936

Shakespear, Lt-Col J., *The Thirty-Fourth Division 1915–1919*, H. F. & G. Witherby, 1921

Simpson, Maj-Gen C. R., *The History of the Lincolnshire Regiment 1914–1918*, Medici Society, 1931

Stacke, Capt H. FitzM., 'The Worcestershire Regiment in the Great War', *The Worcestershire County*, 1928

Stair Gillon, Capt., *The K.O.S.B. in the Great War*, Thomas Nelson and Sons, 1930

———, *The Story of the 29th Division*, Thomas Nelson & Sons, 1925

Stewart, Col H., *Official History of New Zealand's Effort in the Great War: The New Zealand Division 1916–19*, Whitcombe & Tombs, 1921

Stewart, Lt-Col J., and Buchan, John, *The Fifteenth (Scottish) Division 1914–1919*, Blackwood, 1926

Wood, Maj W. de B., *The History of the King's Shropshire Light Infantry in the Great War 1914–1918*, Medici Society, 1925

Wright, Capt P. L., *The First Buckinghamshire Battalion 1914–1919*, Hazell, Watson & Viney, 1920

Wylly, Col H. C., *The Green Howards in the Great War*, (Richmond, Yorks), 1926

Wyrall, Everard, *The Die-Hards in the Great War*, Harrison & Sons, n.d.

———, *The Gloucestershire Regiment in the War 1914–1918*, Methuen & Co. Ltd, 1931

———, *The History of the 19th Division 1914–1918*, Edward Arnold & Co., ?1939

———, *The History of the Duke of Cornwall's Light Infantry 1914–1919*, Methuen & Co, 1932

———, *The History of the Fiftieth Division 1914–1919*, Percy Lund, Humphries & Co., 1939

———, *The History of the Somerset Light Infantry (Prince Albert's) 1914–1919*, Methuen & Co., 1927

———, *The West Yorkshire Regiment in the War 1914–1918*, Bodley Head, n.d.

Wyrall, Everard, (finished by Synge), *The History of the King's Regiment (Liverpool) 1914–1919*, 3 vols, Edward Arnold & Co., 1935

Unpublished papers and records

Public Records Office, Kew
WO95/14 and WO95/15, GHQ Diaries
WO95/1788, Report of Operations (11th Division)
WO95/1790, Actions of the 32nd, 33rd and 34th Brigades (11th Division)
WO95/2191, Account of Operations (24th Division)
WO95/2312, Inquiry (30th Division)
WO95/2429, Report of Operations (33rd Division)
WO95/2492, Narrative of Operations (36th Ulster Division)
WO95/2513, Report on Operations (37th Division)
WO95/2566, Reports on Operations (39th Division)
WO95/2746, Messages (48th Division)
WO95/2754, Narrative of Operations,143rd Inf. Bde (48th Division)
WO95/2987, Reports on Operations (58th Division)
WO95/3010, War Diary of 177th Bde (59th Division)
WO95/3095, Operations and Events (63rd (RN) Division)
WO95/3159, Operations (1st Australian Division)
WO95/3444, Report on Operations (4th Australian Division)
WO95/3786, Summary of Operations (2nd Canadian Division)
WO95/3839, Summary of Operations (3rd Canadian Division)
WO95/3881, Summary of Operations (4th Canadian Division)

Meteorological Office, Bracknell:
Forecast Books of Colonel E. Gold, Meteorologist to the BEF.

INDEX

Compiled by the Author